How to Build a Highly Profitable Martial Arts School

Build Run Scale

Dervish Dervish

6th Degree Master Black Belt, BSc, PGCE

Learn more about how Dervish Dervish can help your school here

Dedication

I would like to dedicate this book to my three fantastic children, Chloe, Harry, and Jack. I love you all so much. You can achieve anything you want if you set your mind to it. Be the best you can be.

Acknowledgements

I would like to thank my wife, Kim, for supporting me in writing this book. She told me I had a wealth of knowledge on how to run a successful martial arts school and encouraged me to put it down on paper.

I would also like to thank my mentors, Roy Inman and Nick Thorpe, for strongly suggesting that I write a book to help future instructors develop their schools and introduce more people to martial arts.

A special thank you to the editorial team at Book Publishing Company, particularly Cheryl Ann, who streamlined the entire process and guided me every step of the way.

Over the past 15 years, I have invested in many business mentors because I understand the immense impact they have. Their guidance, encouragement, and accountability have shaped me into the person I am today. Without them, I would not have embarked on this journey of personal development, business growth, and entrepreneurship. There are too many to name, but I must acknowledge Jeff Smith and Stephen Oliver, who played a significant role in helping me take my school to the next level.

Finally, I want to acknowledge you, the reader, you have invested in this book and given me your most valuable asset, time. I hope it provides you with far greater value than its cost. By choosing to read these words, you have already set yourself apart from the pack. You have the potential to turn your school into something truly great.

CONTENTS

Part 1
INTRODUCTION

Chapter 1

Who This Book Is For and What You Can Get From It

This book is for those driven instructors who want to offer a quality service and make a lifelong impact on their students, all while making a great professional living.

This book is full of information for martial arts instructors at various stages of their school's life journey. I'm confident that if you're deciding to open up a school, you will find massive value. Or, if you run a long-established school and want to earn a better income doing what you love, you will also massively benefit.

This book is for those who may be victims of their own success—your classes are full, you're making 'good' money, but you know there's a better way.

This book is for those who are willing to learn, and it's definitely not for those who are nay-sayers.

I know that from reading this book, you will gain lots of ideas and processes that you can implement into your school, which in turn will help its success. It will be an eye-opener that demonstrates that being paid very well for running your school professionally, with your students' best interests at heart, is all down to you and how you create amazing, unmatched value within your programme.

I say this throughout the book, but your school's success is 100% dependent on your willingness to read what's contained within these pages and then create an action plan to implement. I tell all my mentees that Action = Results. I expect, though, that because you're reading this, you're already a step ahead of the others—so well done on wanting to become even better.

We may or may not have spoken before, but if you like what you read and want to exponentially grow your school, just reach out. Email me at hello@DervishMentoring.com. I run a select group masterminding programme and 1:1 mentoring for martial arts school owners who want to build a profitable business whilst delivering an amazing service. I am a serial property investor too and hold a property mastermind and mentoring programme. If you are an accomplished martial arts business owner and have thought about investing in property but are unsure how to go about it, I can definitely help you with that.

I do hope that you find lots of value in the book and that you start to grow your business.

Good luck.

Dervish Dervish

6th Degree Black Belt

Chapter 2

You're a Karate Man, I Do a Different Style So, What You're Telling Me Won't Work

When I first started to read about the very successful schools—those with amazing retention, effective marketing, the ability to enrol 15+ students a month, and growth of 10, 20, or even 30 students per month, while maintaining a high standard and making a good profit—I was a little hesitant. I would frequently make excuses, such as, 'Well, they do tae-kwon-do, so it's different,' or say things like, 'Yes, but that's BJJ, and that's all the rage now.' I'd tell myself, 'Well, it's different for them because they live in the South, and there's more money there.' Another excuse I made was, 'But they're a 4th Dan, and I'm only a 2nd Dan.' I would tell myself all sorts of things to mask why they were successful and I wasn't. It was absolute nonsense. My mindset was all wrong; I had massive self-limiting beliefs.

The truth of the matter is that it doesn't matter what you teach—whether you are a traditional karate style, tai-chi, or krav maga, what grade you are, or anything else. What ultimately matters is how you position and run your school and how you service your students. If you are a 1st-degree Black Belt or have been training for 3-4 years, you know the main differences between Judo and Karate, or Ju-Jitsu and Aikido. But remember, you're looking at it through a martial artist's eyes. When a parent contacts your school, they have no idea what the difference is between the various martial arts. If we asked 100 parents what the difference is between the different martial arts, they wouldn't be able to say much. To them, they all seem the same. This is the same for your grade or your competition record.

Can You Help Them?

All they want to know is, 'Can you help me solve a problem?'—that is what all businesses do: solve problems. They are only bothered about what you can do for them, and that's not a bad thing because if you can help them, your business will grow. The problem they may have is that they want their child to listen more at home, to stop answering back, to gain more confidence, to burn some energy, and so on. As a martial arts teacher, you should be able to help with all of those things, plus much more.

You must look at your school like a business. The more seriously you treat your business, the more successful it will become. If you treat it like a hobby, then it will cost you like a hobby. If you treat it like a business, then it will pay you like one.

Even when I started to attend courses and seminars, I was still a bit hesitant and very sceptical about it all. I would always think, 'No, they just want to sell me something, and I'm not being sold to.' I'd then go back to my school and continue doing the same things I had been doing, obviously not getting anywhere, other than treading water. Looking back, it was my mindset that was all wrong. Rather than going into it thinking, 'OK, these guys are doing better than me, I need to learn as much as I can' (like you would do if these people were technically better than you in your art), I was thinking they were all watering down their art and overcharging.

You need to understand this from the get-go: if you are truly offering a professional product that makes life-changing improvements to your students, then you should be paid properly for that. I don't know how many students I didn't teach or how many thousands of pounds my business didn't make because I sat on the fence for about 8-10 years, pondering whether to invest in a mentor. Don't make my mistake and prevent your life from getting better. Don't sit on the fence and ponder.

When you are reading the following chapters, please remember that I have been in your position. I started from scratch, didn't have any loans to get the business going, didn't have any mentors, and the worst thing—I thought I could do it all on my own. I honestly don't know why I carried on during my first year. The number of times it ended up costing me to go and teach was unreal. My expenses were constantly higher than my income, and that is no way to grow a business. Regardless of your style, grade, lineage, age, or experience, I can help you grow your school to levels you wouldn't have thought possible. If you are a 1st Dan Black Belt or a Master 7th or 8th Black Belt, I will be able to help your school grow.

In summary, I can guarantee that if you read this book with an open mind—and this is the most important part—IMPLEMENT the strategies, then you will see your school improve as a business, both professionally and financially.

Dervish Dervish

Chapter 3

Do You Run a Gym, a Club, an Academy or a Professional School

Before we continue, I think it will be best to explain that I will be referring to your 'gym', 'club', or 'academy' as 'school' from now on. This is part of the correct terminology puzzle you need to change immediately. In 2004, I opened a Karate 'club' as a part-time venture, but as I started to learn more and more about running it successfully and invested in professional mentors, it evolved into a thriving, profitable 'school'.

Calling your 'gym-club-academy-studio' a 'school' will help further separate you from others and raise your value. I expand on this more in the book. Initially, you may not want to, but when you hear parents referring to your following as a school, it really helps lift your professionalism. The more professional your operation, the more your parents will appreciate it, the more your profits will grow.

Dervish Dervish

Chapter 4

How I Was Making £100,000 per Year in Primary Schools but Was Missing Out on at Least £250,000

Back when I started treating my little karate 'club' as a business, I thought to myself, 'Why don't I try to earn some money teaching karate before my lessons start in the evenings?' It seemed like a good idea, and I knew that primary schools were always on the lookout for after-school provision. So, back in 2008, I sent out some very basic-looking A4 letters to about 15 local primary schools. This was before I started reading about marketing, so believe me, these letters were very bad. Here are some of the mistakes I made:

- I did not target schools in high demographic areas.

- I didn't track the letters.

- I didn't send multiple letters to different members of staff.

- I had no scheduled follow-up system.

- The content of the letter was a single A4 sheet, which was probably all about me and how I could help them with their fitness and self-defence (another mistake).

There was nothing strategic about the approach. I simply sent letters and waited for them to contact me; I gave them all the control. I suppose, looking back, I was very lucky to even get a response, but one of the themes you'll hopefully pick up throughout this book is: Action equals results. I did something, albeit not professional and planned out, but nonetheless, it got results.

If you are ever thinking that you're not getting enough new students or that you're not growing as quickly as you would like, then you need to change things, because whatever you're doing at the moment isn't working as well as it should. I am very confident that if you started to do just 2-3 new things to market your school, you would grow your membership base. Likewise, if you did 2-3 simple things aimed at keeping students longer, your net enrolment and gross income would increase.

After sending out that huge (or so I thought) marketing blast of 15 envelopes containing a single-page letter and moaning about how much I had spent on stamps, I somehow managed to secure an appointment at a local school. They emailed me and wanted to know more about how we could start in their school. Wrongly, I didn't pounce on the opportunity, and I think I replied about 2-3 days later. Whenever a lead comes into your system, you should follow up ASAP. From what I remember, I didn't practice what I was going to say, and I definitely didn't have any sales pitch planned. They must have liked me, because I managed to get a 12-week (1 term) booking.

When we started in this school, I didn't even ask for them to recommend our programme. But it was a teacher from a local school who was in their 'cluster' and just happened to be attending the monthly cluster meeting on a day I was teaching. I didn't know anything about her seeing my lesson, but she left a message with the office asking me to get in touch. I followed up (probably not as quickly or as professionally as I could) and, after another meeting, I had another 12-week contract. I thought to myself, 'I've just added an extra £130, approximately, to my weekly gross.' So, from sending 15 letters, I had managed to secure 24 lessons. If I remember correctly, I was charging £69 per hour, which I thought was absolute top-end. Being paid £69 per hour for teaching karate at 24 years old was amazing, I thought.

Another mistake was that I was comparing myself to a normal football or gymnastics teacher and not valuing what I did. When I realised the true value of our programme, I raised our rates accordingly. In 2022, our prices started at £139 per hour for school-funded lessons, and for parent-funded lessons, they ranged from £150 to £250 per hour (depending on how many students booked on). If you are reading that and thinking, 'What? No way! How is that even possible?' it's about demonstrating the true value of your programme and separating yourself from 'just another sports club being delivered by a normal sports coach'.

For instance, when a prospect first contacts your school and visits for the first time, they need to think, 'Wow, this is amazing; this is going to help my child in so many ways.' You want the school teachers or head teachers to see that you are not just some other sports coach who has done a 6-week training course and can now teach children. We are professional martial arts instructors who teach children amazing, transferable LIFE SKILLS.

As the years went on, I didn't really start to market any more strategically, but I began to realise more and more that I could deliver a before-school lesson and an after-school lesson. I could then easily make over £200 for about 2 hours' work. Multiply that by 5 days a week, and I was making over £1000 just from primary schools. I could also get to the gym easily during the day and do any other 'low-value' errands during the school day. If you do want to work with me and we get to work together, I will explain low-value and high-value tasks. As an entrepreneur we always need to spend our time on the high- value tasks, tasks that improve your business the most.

I really did think, though, that £1000 per week for a 26-28-year-old was great. However, I was too short-sighted. Again, I wasn't seeing the true value of this, and I continued to market to more and more schools until I was absolutely fully booked. In 2014, I took on my first-ever full-time instructor. He was to shadow me, and then, as more and more primary schools came on board, he was to take on those. It wasn't long before he had a full-time primary school schedule. As I started to learn more and more about marketing, I streamlined my marketing to primary schools and continued to layer on touchpoints, which then resulted in an increase in leads and work. I then employed a 3rd and 4th full-time Sensei.

I Was Looking at It All Wrong

It all sounds good, doesn't it? But I was only seeing the yield per hour instead of the true value. At our peak, we were probably grossing around £2,500–£3,000 per week, which is about £100,000 per year, just in our primary school work. This was brilliant, and it wasn't to be snubbed at. The business really started to grow, and it was great moving from school to school, seeing all of my branded suits being worn in the borough.

However, I used to refer to this side of the business as the "icing on the cake." Our primary school work was just something we did on the side, and it was not the core element of our business. I loosely tracked metrics but nothing like drop rates, LTV (lifetime value) for each school, percentage of the group who grade at the end of every term, etc. If I knew then what I know now, I would have engineered it all completely differently. I would have designed and implemented a systemised marketing plan, gone into select primary schools, and got them to attend our Karate School so they could see exactly how beneficial our tuition was for their child. Our LTV for each student would have doubled and more than likely tripled.

Conditioning Parents

As I learned more and more about building a successful business and understanding that the hardest thing to do is get a client, I realised that the primary school work should be seen as a stepping stone into full enrolment in our karate school. I had engineered it, though, so that students and parents were being conditioned to think that taking part in karate in their school was good enough. In previous years, we had been training parents to think of us "just like another before/after school club." Some parents would call us up and say, "Well, breakfast club is only £2, why are you charging £6, £7, £8?" We used to do staff training on how to explain that breakfast club is where children have a slice of toast, play with Lego, or do some colouring, and the teacher is in the room but by no means teaching them anything—it's not a unique character development programme being delivered by a professional martial artist who is teaching transferable LIFE SKILLS.

Every now and then, we would run special offers to try to get students to attend, but it wasn't systemised or strategic. It was more of an off-the-cuff approach. If you are wanting to build a scalable, profitable business, then everything needs to be systemised, and nothing should be "off the cuff." Compared to our 2008–2016 days, we started to systematically attract students to our school. We had some very successful conversion rates, and when you looked at the fact that rather than paying £6–£7 per hour (another stupid mistake—we lowered our fees because we were in primary schools and had no facility overheads!), we could get them to our school, and they would be paying at least £15 per lesson, moving up to £25 for our highest-end programme. Students were worth twice and maybe even three or four times more as members of our martial arts school.

We had a moral obligation to educate parents just how crucial our programme was to their child's development. If you are doing one lesson a week in school, it is good, but enrolling into our martial arts school is by far better. Your child's LIFE SKILL journey will exponentially increase. Once parents did attend, they were always glad. Yes, it was dearer, and it wasn't as convenient as their primary school, but it was such a better experience for their child.

How Did We Get Them to Our Karate School?

From 2019, we used to run lots of events at our school for primary school children, including:

- Orientation days

- Board breaking confidence seminars

- Goal setting seminars

- Belt graduations

- Movie days

- Seasonal parties

- Plus much more

The aim was to get the students and parents through our doors and wow them with the experience.

Introduce Positive Touchpoints

We also used to make welcome calls to the parents and send out welcome letters. If you are wanting to grow a successful business, you must always think to yourself, "How can I stand out?" I can 99% guarantee that they won't be getting any handwritten letters from their football, rugby, swimming, or netball coaches, and they certainly won't be getting "update on your child's progress" calls from their coach. We constantly need to stand out and make positive touchpoints.

If you are a parent, just ask yourself: When was the last time a coach from your child's activity called you to give you an update on their progress? Or sent you a handwritten letter to say thank you for your continued support? Or wrote them a Happy Birthday card? Or made a personal Happy Birthday call? From my experience, they tend to text or email reminding you when payment is due. If you've had similar connections, then how does that make you feel?

If you want to catapult your enrolment, you need to go to where your target audience is. For most of you, that is primary schools. You need to market to them, start a relationship, deliver a programme at their school, and then attract them to your school. It is a lot easier for them to enrol in your school after they have done 5-6 lessons at their primary school. You have introduced them to your amazing programme, and you have educated parents on the benefits of training with you.

This is not the place for me to explain the intricacies of working in primary schools, but doing this will catapult your enrolment. Don't be one of those instructors who says, "I've got no time." There are 24 hours in a day; sleep 8 at most (I'm a 7-hour man). You've then got 16 hours to do all your other tasks. We each have 1,440 minutes in a day—what are we doing with them? My mentees find a way, or they find an excuse. As a Martial Artist, I expect you are not an excuses person.

In summary, earning good money in primary schools is better than nothing but it should be seen as a stepping stone into full enrolment at your school. Getting students to enrol into your school will really grow your active count.

Chapter 5

Get Your Mindset Right Plan for and Expect Your School to Be Successful

Whether You Think You Can or Think You Can't, You're Right

Success in your school, like most things in life, is down to your mindset. The famous Henry Ford quote is: *'Whether you think you can or think you can't, you're right.'* Throughout this book, you will be presented with lots of ideas that you may or may not believe will work. If you believe they won't work, then you probably won't implement them. Or, if you think you'll just 'give it a go,' you will put in minimum effort and then claim it doesn't work (it will become a self-fulfilling prophecy).

Looking at it from a positive mindset, if you say it will work and go 100% into implementing everything, I can personally guarantee it will work if you are doing it correctly. The ideas and strategies I share here in this book, and with my mentees, work because I have implemented them all.

Truly Believe in Yourself

Believe you can professionalise your school so it is the best in your area. Believe you can make a professional income from doing a professional job. Believe in the endless benefits your programme has to offer and how you positively impact students' lives. Believe that your school can provide well for your family. Believe you can build it into a successful business. Believe you are capable.

Your Mind Is the Biggest Obstacle or Asset to Your Growth

I have read lots of books on mindset, and they all have a common theme: Do you have a fixed mindset or a growth mindset? Reading this as a martial artist, you are likely to have a growth mindset. You started your art as a white belt, or equivalent, i.e. a beginner. As your training evolved, so did your skill set and proficiency in applying these skills.

You may, though, only have a growth mindset in your art because you are now highly trained and are considered a Master to the outside world. You may have forgotten your clumsy, uncoordinated beginner days because they are that far gone. You may have forgotten getting thrown around a lot in sparring or struggling to learn Katas/forms.

For anything new you start, you may throw your hands in the air and say, 'I can't do it.' We used to teach our students a concept of *'the power of yet.'* Whenever they would say, 'Sensei, I can't do this kick,' we would then say, 'Let's rephrase this – I can't do this kick YET, but I'm learning how to do it.'

This is the mindset you need throughout this book. When you are reading new concepts, you must think to yourself, *'Ok, I can't do this yet, but I will learn how to.'* Your mind is the biggest obstacle or asset to your growth.

One of my mentors used to say, *'The skillset without the correct mindset will leave you upset.'* I believe he picked it up from a book he read, so unfortunately, I cannot give credit to the author. However, what a brilliant saying. My mindset has massively changed over the past 15 years. I was the classic scarcity mindset rather than the abundance mindset. I was hesitant to try new things because I was scared of wasting money. I used to think, *'Well, I*

could spend £200 on this, and I might not get anything back.'
Instead, I should have been thinking that if we implement this new
idea, it could help our retention, enrolment, standard, profitability,
etc.

Implementing the Concepts for Growth

By implementing the concepts in this book, you will start to see
improvements and growth in all elements of your school's
operations. Truly believe that success is out there waiting for you,
and all you need to do is aim for it, work hard (don't forget that bit),
and it will come.

I'm not going to lie to you – you do have to work hard to keep your
school full. The hard work comes at the beginning when you are
starting to get traction on the new ideas. But when you have
momentum, you need to keep it going. Research the great speaker
Zig Ziglar and his *'prime the pump'* example. It explains that to
pump water from a well, it takes a lot of hard work at the beginning
without any noticeable results. But once the water starts to flow, it's
easy to keep it flowing if you maintain the action. This is exactly the
concept you need to think of when starting your marketing.

Where Do I Start?

During parts of this book, you may feel a bit overwhelmed with
ideas and concepts and be confused about where to start. That is
absolutely normal. My advice to all my mentees is to just do one
thing at once. If you concentrate on bringing 1-2 things in a week,
you will be in a much better place in a year's time. A year may seem
like a long time, but let's agree that the time is going to pass anyway,
so you might as well use it to improve your business and your life.

By the end of a 12-month period, you could have easily brought in +45 actions that will have improved your school. If we do end up working together, & I hope we do, I have a plan of actions you should implement at first to get you the furthest, the quickest. I want my mentees to achieve great results within 6 weeks of working with me. Like always, though, you need to work.

Avoiding the Excuse of Being Too Busy

Don't ever give yourself the excuse that you are too busy. Are you too busy to improve your life? Are you too busy to create a business that can provide you with a good profit and handsome dividends? There are 24 hours in a day, most people sleep 8, leaving you with 16 hours for work, family time, building your business, etc. I would suggest blocking out unnegotiable time to work on your business, e.g. every morning from 5-6.30am or every evening from 7-8.30pm. You get the idea. Those little 90-minute daily slots will add up, and you will see improvements.

Enjoy the book, and I hope that we work together in the future so I can help you improve your school and build your ideal life.

Part 2
FUNDAMENTALS

Dervish Dervish

Chapter 6

The Basics You Need To Understand Enrol A Student And Keep Them!

Your number one aim in running your martial arts school is to enrol a student and then keep them (forever). If you understand that and bring it to every element of your business, then you will be more successful.

In simplistic terms, you should be applying Pareto's principle here: 80% of your time should be spent getting and retaining new clients, and 20% should be dedicated to the other elements. It's not a hard and fast rule; you might spend 70% on getting and retaining new clients and 30% on other tasks. What I want you to understand is that your marketing really needs to increase. Your goal is to spend a large part of your week marketing your school to gain new members.

It does not matter how good your style is, how great a teacher you are, what your lineage is, what your competition record is like, or how bad the instructor down the street is. The only thing that matters is enrolling a student and keeping them for as long as possible. A great way to do this is to help every student, once they enrol, set and achieve goals, and become a better person as a result of your programme (much more on this later).

They Are a Lower Grade and Have More Students than Me

When I first started teaching just over 25 years ago, I remember one of my instructors lamenting how the other karate club was getting all these members, even though he was a lower grade, hadn't been to the English championships, and was teaching all the katas wrong. I don't think the other guy was teaching all the katas wrong; he was probably teaching what his instructor taught him. Looking back now, after building and running my own very profitable karate school, I realise that the other karate club was just the same as this instructor's club – their dropout rate was somewhere between terrible and horrendous. They had no real enrolment process and only taught physical skills.

But they did two things to get new students (which was double what the other instructor was doing). My business mentors told me that it wasn't really that hard to stand out in our industry because most instructors are too scared to spend money on enrolling new students (more on that later) and don't treat their school like a business; they treat it like a hobby. The fact that you are reading this means you are not in that camp, so well done. They believe that if they are good at their art and have a good competition record, then students will flood to their school. Wrong! The fact that you are reading this means you don't want to treat your school like a hobby or be an amateur business owner. You know you can achieve more.

Treat Your School like A Business and Not a Hobby

In business, the number one aim should be to gain a customer and keep them forever. Ideally, because you offer a truly unique programme and they feel valued, they will recommend more customers, who, in turn, will recommend more customers. Running a martial arts school is no different. If you treat your martial arts class/club like a hobby, then it will cost you like a hobby. If you treat it like a business and learn how to run that business properly, it will start to pay you like a business. You must understand that teaching excellent lessons is only a small part of running a successful school.

Now, getting a student is easier said than done. It's not as hard as the small clubs make it out to be, but later in this book, I will identify many methods of attracting students to your school. Before we get to the marketing section, though, I'll let you in on a little secret: there is no one amazing marketing trick or hack, no 'this will get you 300 students in a month' pill. The truth is, you need to do loads of marketing. Never just rely on doing one thing to gain students – that is business sabotage. As a business owner, you have to work hard on keeping your school full. It is a never-ending task; it cannot be completed, only maintained.

Get a Student and Keep Them Forever Mindset

So, if you want to run a profitable business, of course, teach high-value lessons and provide the best service you can, but underpinning all of that must be a 'get a student and keep them forever' mindset. When you have a team, they need to understand this concept too. Their role is not to just turn up to class, teach, and then go home. Their role is to help market your school to gain new members and to keep hold of your existing ones.

In summary, when you understand that your primary role is to attract students. And your secondary role is to teach, you will start to grow. To be successful, you must be in the business of attracting new students and keeping them for as long as possible.

Dervish Dervish

Chapter 7

Forget About Your Competition If You Want To Be The Best

I do not know your area, but if it's anything like most areas in the country, it will have a lot of small, part-time martial arts 'clubs' that do zero marketing. They may put a badly designed banner outside the venue they hire, but that doesn't count as advertising, and many are barely breaking even. In my area, there were over 30 martial arts clubs. I didn't live in a big city—just an average-sized town with a population of about 220,000. Some of these may even be losing money every month, but they don't see that because they are volunteering their time.

You may then have one professional school that is the big player in the area. They are the 'Google' of martial arts in your area, the 700-pound gorilla. They are the one that all the other 'broke' martial arts instructors often call. They are the one that everybody seems to know about, but believe me, not everybody in your area knows about them. You will know about them because you see them as the biggest school or club in your area. They are your number one competition for getting students.

From the outside looking in, they seem to be running a brilliant operation. You may even guiltily admire what they have done. They may have a big following, their own nice venue with lots of passing traffic, their classes are always full, and they are open 5, 6, or 7 days a week. When you're reading this, you may be thinking of the school I'm describing. You need to forget about them because you're in your own lane and are going to take your school exactly where you want it to be. You are not going to copy them because that's not you.

The school I am describing may actually be your school. You may be the 700-pound gorilla. If so, congratulations—I am still confident there is a lot of hidden profit in your operation.

Charge What You're Worth, Not What You Think People Will Pay

One thing you need to do is not be bothered at all about what your so-called competition is charging. I fell for this trap when opening my karate school (at the time, though, it was a bog-standard karate 'club'; it evolved into a school over the next 20 years). What they are charging is what they think they are worth. You need to charge what you are worth.

My first mistake was to open up far away from other karate clubs. Now, in theory, that sounds good, but the only problem was that I opened up in the middle of nowhere. The local primary school was over 2 miles away and was tiny (it had 2 years in one class rather than the typical 30 students in one year standard). The area I chose to move into was pretty much rural. It wasn't a town or even a small gathering of houses; it was an area on a main road that led from one small town to another, even smaller town.

That was one of many mistakes I would make over the next 10 years until I started learning about business and how to run a successful martial arts school. My reasoning for opening there was that if I wasn't near anybody else, then I would get the business. But I stupidly did not take into consideration the non-existent population of the area and, in doing so, sabotaged my business before it even got going. I hope that from reading this book, you'll realise I've made lots of mistakes, but one thing I kept doing was learning and improving.

I remember ringing up the 3 closest karate clubs in the nearest town, pretending to be interested in lessons, and asking them how much their lessons were. At the time, they were £4.50-£5 for one hour. After serious contemplation on matters I knew nothing about (such as creating value, setting yourself apart, price elasticity, and price psychology), I decided £4 for 1.5 hours would be what I charged.

My stupid reasoning was, "Well, if I'm a whole 50p cheaper and they're getting 30 minutes more, then they'll be queuing up for my excellent lessons." Wrong! That 50p, even adjusted for inflation, wasn't a big differentiator. Looking back, all I did was encourage parents to 'dump and run'. Parents didn't want to sit and watch their child being taught for 90 minutes; they used that time to do a few errands. They could go to the shops or pick up or drop off their other child, etc. I could have been delivering the best lessons ever, but the parents weren't there to see it. In effect, I was just a babysitter who happened to teach their children karate.

Don't Be the Cheapest or Even Second-Cheapest Around

It was only after years of reading about business, learning about price psychology, being in mastermind groups, and having a mentor (the best investment I ever made in myself and business) that I realised that pricing yourself even in the same region puts you in the same bracket as your competition. To your prospects, you are just the same as them, even if you are 10 times better.

If there's one thing I urge you to do, it's NOT to be the cheapest around—not even in the same range. Do not be in a race to the bottom. With price, there is a perception of value. If you're charging just 10, 20, or 30% more than the nearest competitor, then you're not really standing out.

Look at it this way: are parents going to think you're massively different from others because you are £2 or £3 dearer per lesson (roughly £25 more per month)? I was proud to be the dearest karate school around. I remember one parent saying to me on the phone, "We know you're the dearest around, but I've spoken to my husband, and we know you are professional and get results." That put a big smile on my face. I mentioned this in team meetings and team training many times.

Think of it this way: do you want to be the Rolls Royce of tuition or the pound shop of tuition? Not everybody wants to buy the cheapest of everything. Have a look at the items you buy: do you buy the absolute cheapest budget items—clothes, food, cosmetics, cars, etc.? Besides, you don't want to be targeting those who look for the cheapest of everything.

One thing I learned after running my own school for 20 years and teaching over 10,000 students and meeting thousands of parents is that those who pay the least value what you do the least. They also provide you with the most headaches. On the flip side, those who pay you the most value your service the most.

Learn From Your Competition—But Only If They're Smashing It

All your competition is doing is what their Sensei did—give or take 10%. More often than not, they make changes to the technical syllabus, but not to the business systems. They think that because their 'club' has been around since the 1970s or 1980s, they have a solid reputation in the community and that everybody knows about them.

I was speaking to one of my karate friends about 5 years ago, and they were saying that now they have taken over, they can finally start teaching a kata this particular way, bring in these basic combinations, and deliver warm-ups this way. Doing those things are great, and I am not belittling those types of choices, but what I am saying is that don't think that by bringing in a fancy new kata or some new basic combinations (or different style warm-ups) that you used to do during the 'good old days' will suddenly flood your school with new students.

Building a good, strong martial arts school with a steady flow of white belts and a minimal dropout rate takes much more than high-energy classes and a new form or two. Building your school means marketing your school is your number one priority, closely followed by retaining those students. All your team needs to understand that their role is to promote and market the school—not just teach lessons. Lessons, of course, need to be engaging, challenging, and develop the students, but your goal is to constantly and never-endingly market your school.

Observe the Masses and Do the Opposite

Only copy your competition if they are absolutely smashing it from a business side of things—not a competition record side of things. When your prospective parents contact you, are they initially contacting you because, even though their child has never done competitions before, they want to be a world champion? No. They are contacting you to see if you can help them with a problem they would like you to solve.

If you want to be the same as all the other martial arts schools, then copy what they are doing. I refer to Warren Buffet's quote: "Observe the masses and do the opposite." If you want to grow a decent school whilst developing students with integrity, determination, discipline, and much more—and earn a living—then follow what the super successful schools do. Don't follow the schools that are part-time and are hardly making a profit.

In summary, success leaves clues. Follow the successful, and success will follow.

Chapter 8

Do Not Just Teach Physical Skills

If you want to be average and earn a little money on the side of your normal day job, then it's absolutely fine to just teach 'kicks and punches', i.e., physical skills.

That is what I set out to do back in 2004 and did so for about 10 years. Just pass on what your instructor taught you and your students won't know any different. I expect, though, that anybody reading this wants more than to just teach 1-2 nights a week and have a little bit of spending money. If you are reading this, you know that you can have more and that you deserve more. You may even know deep down that you are worth more. You don't want to be just another 'run of the mill' standard martial arts club. You want to offer a fantastic programme and be paid well for that provision. You probably want to build something that you are proud of that one day will exceed what you thought was capable with a martial arts school. If that is you, then I get it because I was the same – I had those ambitions and achieved them.

Highlight the Benefits of Regular Martial Arts Training

One of my very successful mentors said that you need to highlight to the parents the benefits of regular martial arts training, far beyond the physical fitness. I was in my 3rd year of university studying sport science, so all my marketing (used very loosely) back in the early 2000s was around the physical benefits of karate. What an absolute waste! You could have placed my so-called 'benefits' list next to any other sports activity and there wouldn't have been much difference. Looking back, I was using words that I thought would 'wow' the parents: muscle fibres, sliding filament theory, ATP, energy systems, dynamic stretching. How embarrassing they were! At the time, though, I just thought this is what parents wanted to hear. Their child was going to be taught by a person with a degree in sport science who was then going to become a lecturer. Yet again, I was wrong. I should have just put up a poster that said, "Karate, £4, Tuesdays 6:30-8pm", simple and straight to the point. I have no doubt that would have pulled better. At that point, though, I did not know the huge impact that industry-specific knowledge would have on my business. I mention 'industry-specific' because I have read many marketing, sales, and business books, and they are good, but nothing compared to when I attended 'industry-specific' programmes and masterminds in America. Their attention to detail allowed me to grow my school to unheard-of heights.

Standing Out from the Local 'Club'

Your programme needs to stand out from the local 'club' down the street. Your professionalism, guestology, atmosphere, and the lesson experience are all factors in this important mix. But one of the biggest ways of doing this is to deliver personal development lessons, often referred to as 'mat chats'. But there is more to a mat chat than just sitting down and talking about whatever the instructor feels they want to talk about. We used to have 'personal development' chats, and each week there was a different theme. The theme was based on a chapter we were covering from a personal development book. To tie into the PD chat, we also had handouts to give every student. These handouts had questions on them that the students could answer to earn character tabs for their belts (more on this later in the book). The handouts were tangible, and students took them home. This created value and separated us from other 'sports'. The handouts were also available on our Google Classroom, again another resource that reinforces our value. The personal development chats were for 4-5 minutes in our trial programme and about 8-10 minutes in our Black Belt programmes. We also had brief You Tube videos explaining each chapter so that parents and children could learn from home.

In combination with our personal development books that were covered each week, we had a 'success quote' which ran for two weeks. The 'success quotes' were displayed on our success wall and posters located around our school. We also had a LIFESKILL of the term, which ran for 6-7 weeks during term time. I will explain these, along with goal-setting sheets, visualisation posters, and book reports in more detail later, but maybe from reading the above you have an idea of how to separate your school so it's not even in the same league as other 'clubs'.

Creating Value and Standing Out to Parents

Parents need to come into your school and genuinely be positively shocked at what you are teaching. You want professional, career-oriented parents to think, 'This stuff will help me in my career. This is really going to give my child a boost in life.' One thing I used to say to parents at various points during their second lesson and enrolment conference was, 'Just think how many of Bob's friends in his class at school are being taught this... think how much he is going to stand out in so many things.' I wanted parents to see that their child was receiving an education that so many others weren't. They needed to understand that we were unique.

Many Moving Parts Contribute to Success

There are so many moving parts to running a successful martial arts school that I don't just want you to think that doing a mat chat every lesson and giving them handouts means you stand out. Having a personal development chat every lesson, combined with self-discipline sheets, success quotes, school results recognition, character tabs, regular progress checks, building rapport with your parents, book reports, graduations, fun events, plus much more, all contribute to you standing out in your community. You also need to fully understand your parents' goals for enrolling their child in your school. If you can genuinely help them, then they will be able to see it. If you can't, then be honest with them. Tell them that you believe we are not a good fit for each other and recommend somewhere else.

Turning Up, Teaching, Leaving is Not How You Grow a School

You cannot expect to just turn up five minutes before your lesson, teach, go home, then do the same for your next lesson and then moan that your school isn't growing. Like a top athlete – the work is done outside the gym, and you are crowned in the arena. You need to do the work outside of your lesson times if you want to run a profitable martial arts school. Teaching the lessons is the easy part; you need to market, market, and then market your school. Marketing your school never ends, just like your physical training and improvement, it cannot be completed.

Quality and Service Should Be Greater than the Charge

Remember, though, that you need to have your students' best interests at heart. Yes, you want to earn money, and there is nothing wrong with that if you are providing an outstanding service. But your parents and students need to see quality. They need to feel valued and see the benefits. The quality and service you provide should be more than what you are charging. You never want people to think they are not getting value for money.

In summary, the developmental piece and LIFE SKILL piece is a major component that will separate you from others and help create more value.

Chapter 9

Do You Run Your School The Same As Your Instructor Did?

Most of the industry run their martial arts 'club' the same as their instructors did, who in turn ran it the same as their instructors did, and so on. If your instructor was highly successful at running their school, had great gross earnings, brilliant retention, and grew their personal net worth each year, then well done – stick with them and do exactly as they did.

If, however, your instructor used to have the same size of class year after year, had another job, didn't really want to develop the club, never marketed, and didn't constantly learn about the industry and implement best business practices, then you are doing the right thing by reading this book. If you do what you've always done, then you will get what you've always got.

This mentality can be applied to most things in your life. If you train the same way you always have, then the benefits level off. If you read as many books as you have always done, your learning will grow at that same level. My advice would be to level up – as soon as you do this, you will see the benefits. Don't follow people who have not achieved that which you wish to achieve.

Back in January 2004, I too ran my Karate 'club' very similarly to my instructor and how other instructors ran theirs. Here's the thing though – if you want to copy people, make sure you copy those who are living the life you want to lead. I stayed with a syllabus very close to that which I was taught while coming up through the grades. I implemented some new techniques and katas, but from a non-martial artist's perspective, there were no clear differences between my 'club' and any other.

We had similar suits, similar belts, and were doing similar techniques – it was very close to all the other karate clubs. That's why, during my first year, I made a profit of about £1,000, which was equivalent to about £20 per week (£10 per day). I know that inflation erodes money, but trust me, back in 2004, making £10 per week teaching karate twice a week was bad business.

For some reason, though, I just kept doing the same thing and, obviously, gaining the same results. I didn't know about Einstein's famous quote then.

Don't Listen to Those Who Have a Full-Time Job

If I were starting all over again, I would run a mile away from any instructor who wanted to give me advice on how to build and run a school if they still had a full-time job and were only teaching two lessons a week. Imagine somebody in the gym who was overweight and clearly not as fit as you aspired to be – would you listen to their training advice or model their behaviours? No!

I have had mentors throughout my life, especially in the past 15 years, and there is one thing you need to understand – follow the people who are more successful than you. Learn from them, pick up their behaviours, and model their attitude. I teach my kids that 'success leaves clues' and 'success is not a straight line.'

Do not listen to the instructor who isn't even breaking even. Regarding mentors, please note that your original Sensei, Sifu, Master, or Coach was your mentor – they just didn't label themselves as such. They shared their knowledge, and as a result, you improved.

Unfortunately, for many people, as soon as they leave formal education – be it secondary school, college, or university – their education stops. If you want to be successful, you need to constantly educate yourself. We may get to work together moving forward, and it will be my mission to make your school a success. If we do not get to work together, then make sure you keep learning from people who have achieved what you want to achieve.

It's Not All About Money?

No, it's not, but you try paying your rent, mortgage, bills, shopping, and car finance with anything other than money – it doesn't work. When people say 'it's not all about money,' I do get what they are saying, but you need money to live in a civilised world. Money is useful where it is useful, and here in the UK, it's very useful.

If you are offering a unique service and have your students' best interests at heart, why should you not earn good money? There's a stigma around teaching martial arts, that you should not earn any money from it, and you should do it for the love of the art. What a load of nonsense!

When the Japanese instructors came over to do gradings in the 70s and 80s, they charged a lot for grading fees, but nobody seems to remember that. What about the best lawyers and medical surgeons in the country? They love their jobs but are not expected to do them for free.

Poppy Cutters

Here in the UK, we have a culture of 'poppy cutters' and disliking people for being successful. I remember buying Karate and Martial Arts magazines and seeing instructors who were doing well. I used to speak to my peers and ask them about that particular person, and they would say stupid things like 'they've sold out' or 'he's not even that good.'

I was only 18 at the time, so I didn't think much of it, but looking back, I should have thought 'hang on, I'm listening to my friend who has about 15 students, still works full-time, but I'm only listening to him because he is a higher grade, while I'm not learning from this other guy who has about 400 students and is teaching as a full-time career.'

If you are thinking 'I don't know if I want to earn money because my instructor didn't,' or even thinking that your instructor would disapprove, get out of your own way. Surround yourself with people who want to see you thrive and become successful. I want to see all my mentees be successful, and I want them to build their ideal life.

You will never become successful if you are surrounding yourself with naysayers. A good book to read or person to follow is Arnold Schwarzenegger. He was a very focused and driven person who surrounded himself with people better than him. He will openly admit to not being a 'self-made' man, and he has had many mentors throughout his successful life.

For you to be successful, you need to have mentors. I have a property portfolio and also mentor property investors. However, I still invest in my own mentors – those who are further along than me.

Design Your School for Success

Design your school so that it is built for success. Please do not just do exactly what your instructor did; only do this if you want to get very similar results to them.

I remember a colleague witnessing one of my yellow and orange belt gradings, and we had 52 students grading. He was in awe because that was bigger than his entire active count (white-black belt).

One of the first Black Belt gradings I had, with my Sensei sitting on the panel, we had more than 28 students grading. That was in about 2017, and my school was far from operating at full capacity. Some of our later gradings had many more higher grades.

Lots of people didn't like me, even though they had never met me. They didn't like the fact that I was the '500lb gorilla' in the town and earning very good money from delivering our excellent martial arts programme. They didn't see the 70+ hour weeks, working weekends, taking work away with me, and missing my child's birthday parties, etc.

As my time management improved, so did my work schedule and profits.

Follow Success

In summary, if you want to build and grow a highly profitable school, you cannot do it by copying what other martial art 'club' owners are doing. You need to follow the successful.

Part 3
IT'S A BUSINESS

Chapter 10

Treat Your School Like A Business

If you treat it (your business) like a hobby, then it will cost you like a hobby; treat it like a business and it will pay you like a business.

So many instructors start their 'clubs' because they love their art, and it seems like fun to teach and earn a bit of extra money on the side. Most instructors have a full-time job and teach 1-2 times per week—that's what I did back in 2004. I had a full-time job for the first 7-8 years after opening my school.

Here's the thing though: if you want to build it into a substantial business that will pay you a professional salary and nice dividends, then you can't be working in a full-time job too. Don't get me wrong, you can build it up to a certain level while being in full-time employment, but there is a tipping point. For me, that tipping point was about 120-130 active students, approximately £12k per month.

Now or Never

One of the venues I was hiring twice a week decided to change our agreement from paying for the Monday evening and Saturday up until 3pm, to charging per hour. Now, I can understand their reasoning; they saw how healthy my classes were and thought, 'He can afford it,' especially since the other groups had tiny class sizes. However, they decided that what I was currently paying per day would now be per hour.

So, my Monday night cost would raise from £30 to 3 hours * £30 = £90, and my Saturday cost would also raise from £30 to 6 hours * £30 = £180. So, my rent would go from £90 per week to £270. They did me a favour really, because I decided to take the plunge and rent a commercial unit.

My 12-month lease I signed was approximately £600 per month back in 2010, compared to the £270 per week * 4.2 weeks = £1,134 per month that the other venue wanted to charge for two days a week. As soon as I moved into my own venue, I turned my business learning up a gear and started to devote every hour I possibly could into growing the business.

I was reading about systems, marketing, accounts, customer service, KPIs, KRAs, management, sales, how to build a business, plus much more. I also started to travel to other schools that I thought were successful. Most of the time, they were only marginally better than me; however, if I could pick up 1-2 things to improve my operation, then it was worthwhile. I was obsessed with gaining knowledge.

I have always been focused and driven, but signing a lease for my own premises definitely upped my game.

Treat It Seriously

If you want to build your school into a proper business that is profitable, you need to treat it seriously. You can't just expect to turn up 15 minutes before a lesson twice a week and expect it to exponentially grow—it doesn't work like that.

I do speak to some instructors who want to work with me but then say they don't have time to do anything else. That is absolutely fine, but it just looks like they will stay at the same level they are at. Here are just a few things you should definitely do:

- Have a clear marketing plan

- Have a clear intro process

- Have scripts for initial calls, second lesson calls, and enrolment conferences

- Track your stats (enquiries, first lessons, second lessons, enrolments) daily

- Hold weekly meetings (even if it's just with yourself)

- Hold weekly team training (even if it's just with yourself)

- Have a proper timetable that will allow you to grow

- Maintain good cash flow

- This deserves another reminder: MARKET YOUR SCHOOL

The above are just a small sample of processes you should implement in order to professionalise your school. I explain some of these later in the book. There are many more you will implement as your school grows and as you work with me, but the above are absolute fundamentals to running an efficient and professional business. I will explain them a little more in the following pages.

Chapter 11

Having A Clear Marketing Plan

A single day should not pass in your school when you are not doing at least one thing to attract new members. I mentioned it earlier, but your job is to enrol and keep a student—you continually need to market your school.

Remember the saying: 'You run the day, or the day runs you.' If you don't have a marketing plan, then don't get stuck in analysis paralysis by thinking of everything you need to do—just start off with broad strokes. You could say, 'Well, all this month I'm going to call primary schools in my area and ask to deliver school leaflets.' This can then be broken down into:

- Getting the leaflet designed (we can help you with that)

- Creating a list of primary schools in a 2-3-4-5-mile radius around your school

- Creating a quick professional sounding script for the phone call

- Organising to drop leaflets at three schools a day (or whatever you can manage at first)

The main thing is implementation, not procrastination. Your marketing plan can be broad strokes at first and then just take small steps in implementation. Action = Results.

You will then start to build on your marketing plan each month. For example, each month you can hold a 'bring a friend' type of event. We used to hold this a week after the graduation. It was a fun-themed week, and students were encouraged to bring their friends to class. These events were often well attended because students were keen to show off their new coloured belts. If they did, they earned 5 additional character tabs for their belt—they had shown leadership, so we awarded them leadership tabs.

You can get your Google business page up to date. Your main business hours should not just be your class times— from a prospective parent's perspective, it will only look like you are open for 2 hours a day, 2-3 days a week (which is a big turn-off). Put your opening hours as 8am-8pm, and you will get more calls.

If you use your personal phone as your work phone, I suggest you get another number for personal use. Every time your old personal phone rings, you can answer it professionally. Never answer it by saying 'hello' followed by a long pause—this is such a sign of amateurism. For example, if I ever answered the phone at the school, I would say: 'Good morning/afternoon/evening, Kaizen-Do Karate, Sensei Dervish speaking, how can I help?'

As the number of leads you gather improves, you can arrange to call five of them a day, every day, until you get them booked in. We left enquiries on a clipboard on our front desk, and they were called every day for a week. After that, they were called once a week for a further three weeks. If we had not spoken to them by the 4-week mark, we added their details to our marketing prospect list. During this time, though, they were still sent physical mail. Please do not be cheap and don't underestimate the impact tangible mail can make.

This is not the marketing section of the book, but I need you to understand that if you do not have a clear marketing plan that gets refined each month, then you are dead in the water. You need to keep filling your school with new students.

In summary, remember that your job and any other team member's job is to market your school. Everybody involved in your school operation needs to attract and keep students.

Dervish Dervish

Chapter 12

Have A Clear Intro Process

Another key process is the journey your students follow, which takes them from initial contact to enrolled member. Any great business has a clear 'sales funnel'. If you want to build a great school, you need to have a well-organised yet simple intro process—i.e., a sales funnel. You need to keep track of your leads throughout the entire process so that nobody slips through the cracks.

The worst mindset you can have is thinking, 'If they like it, they will come back; if not, then we don't really want them as students.' What a load of nonsense. Some people mean to get back in touch because they liked what they saw, but unfortunately, life gets in the way. You may be able to relate, has life ever got in the way for you?

We need to hold their hand during the first two lessons and then continue to hold it during the first five weeks. You need to know what your intro process is so that you have a tighter hold on your enrolments. For example, my team was trained not to let more than 2-3 days pass between a student's first lesson and their second lesson. If you leave it for a week, you are framing the parents to think that this is just another 'club' they do once a week. No! You want them to understand that, just like school, where they go five days a week, for them to reap the benefits you are talking about and are confident at delivering, they need to be attending your school for two lessons a week.

Having a clear intro process where you track them throughout the stages will increase the number of enrolments you achieve. Where focus goes, energy flows. If you are focusing on your pipeline, you will start to see the holes in your bucket. Each week, during our weekly meeting, we looked at the number of: leads, first lessons booked, first lessons attended, second lessons attended, ECs carried out, enrolments, renewal conferences, renewals, and more. Those are the vital statistics of your intro process.

Don't forget that if you are not getting a steady, reliable stream of white belts each and every month, your school is already in decline. If you have a slow enrolment month, you had better make it up the following month; otherwise, that lull/dip feeds through to your renewals and active count.

In summary, having a clear intro process will streamline your school and provide an up-to-date measure of how you are doing at that time.

Chapter 13

Have Scripts For Initial Call, 2nd Lesson Call And Enrolment Conferences

Well-designed and rehearsed scripts will ensure that every lead at every stage of your intro process receives the same information. Scripts also ensure you are controlling the conversation and getting the information you want.

Imagine you make the mistake of employing 16–18-year-olds. This, in itself, is not that bad, but after a few hours of team training, you let them loose on answering your phone. I'm telling you this because, stupidly, this is what I did a couple of times until I realised how important the phone is. The phone is often the first 'tangible' impression a potential customer may get of your school. You may get the best lead-generation leaflets designed ever and have the best website/landing page ever, both of which are good, and they ultimately lead the parent to decide to call your school. They then call up and are spoken to by somebody who isn't very professional, who may introduce slang words, and who won't work with someone to get their first lesson booked because they cannot accommodate the possible intro slots you have available. You have then done all this marketing at a cost to your school to get them to call you, only for them to find out you could not accommodate them. They then contact your less-professional, sub-standard competitor and enrol there, where they only teach kicks and punches. You have spent £100s on getting them to act, (which is the hardest part), only to send them to your competition because the team member who answered the phone was not trained well enough. Yes, this has happened to me, and it still winds me up now. It was, however, 100% my fault. I should have trained them more and continually trained them. I do not want you to make the same mistake. For those of you considering working with me, I will be able to fast-track your success by highlighting to you the biggest, most cost-effective mistakes I have ever made. Trust me, I've made lots.

There needs to be scripts available on your front desk for team members to follow and write down the relevant information from the new lead. You also need to have a second lesson confirmation call that all team members are trained on. Then, the final piece of the enrolment puzzle is to have your enrolment conference script practised and rehearsed so you can say it without having to read off a piece of paper. As we evolved, our enrolment conference terminology was weaved in and out of the first and second lessons numerous times, so that when we actually sat down with both parents after the second lesson, we had covered the most important points and then did the price presentation. To have your scripts nailed down, you need to complete your regular weekly team training and your intense team training days (once every month or once every six weeks). It all boils down to the saying, 'Perfect practice makes perfect'. I discuss team training later, but never assume that once you have trained a team member once, they know it. Just like our physical training, bad habits creep in.

When to Delegate and When Not to Delegate

Each task in your school has an impact value. For example, if the pads are not tidy, then it's not likely to lose you any members. However, if your entire school is a mess, that will result in losing members. The impact of the phone is absolute. Following the phone call, you want the parent to say to their spouse, 'They were nice, they really helped me, I've got a good feeling about this, I think Bob will really enjoy it.' You don't want them to say to their spouse, 'Wow, that was bad, I didn't book in, so I'll just book them into somewhere else.' You have done all the legwork by getting them to take action and call you, but yet because you were terrible on the phone, your so-called 'competition' is going to get the business.

Chapter 14

Track Your Stats Daily

Tracking Your Stats

Just like in any sporting competition, you need to keep score so you know who has won or lost. In your business, you need to 'keep score'. This means tracking your stats.

At the end of every shift, you need to track the figures for the day. The most important metrics are:

- Number of enquiries,
- Number of first lessons,
- Number of second lessons,
- Number of ECs,
- Number of enrolments,
- £ Initial investments paid today.

You need to track this so you can project the week and month. These stats also highlight whether you are growing or declining (there is no plateau). Don't get bogged down in this; at first, just write it down on a piece of paper every day. Create a table for the week and fill in each day as it happens. As you bring in the practice, you will start to expand on the process, but before layering on any depth, just concentrate on the above crucial stats. If you have a small team, then encourage an email template you have designed to be sent to you, and the figures can be uploaded to a Google Drive spreadsheet. Having the Google Drive spreadsheet is good because you can monitor your school's stats, even if a team member forgot to send the email.

Tracking your stats means you are looking at them frequently during the week. It forces you to act, because if the charts are heading downwards, you know that your business needs work. I tell my mentees, 'Major in major things.' If they are concentrating on the stats of their school, then they know the major elements. When you start to compile stats, you will then be able to see the weaknesses in your school. For example, you might not be getting enough enrolments simply because you are not getting enough leads, or you might be getting lots of leads, but nobody is enrolling.

Knowing your stats for your school is knowing the pulse of your school.

Chapter 15

Hold Weekly Meetings

Even if you are a one-man/woman operation, still hold weekly meetings. This is so you can reflect on the previous week and make changes for the coming week. During this meeting, you are first and foremost covering the stats. It also keeps team members in the loop. They need to understand that their job is not just to turn up five minutes before a class, teach, and then leave. They should be helping with marketing and retention at a minimum. Teaching, I always found, was the easiest part of running a school, but regardless, your team needs to be accountable for enrolling and retaining students.

Holding team meetings is like telling them the scores of recent sports matches. If we had five first lessons and five second lessons, then that was good because whatever was happening during the first lesson was effective in getting a 100% return/show rate for the second lesson. If we then had zero ECs, it meant they were not ready, and important things were not being covered in the intro or the second lesson confirmation call. We may not have enrolled them because they may not have answered the second lesson confirmation call, looked at the second lesson webpage and video, completed their white belt self-discipline sheet, or had all the adult support network there. You can only analyse this if you have the stats and carry out team meetings and training.

During these meetings, you also go over other items such as:

- Attendance cards – comb through the entire student body to see who may need extra help and/or see whose attendance is waning.

- New members – make sure all team members know who they are and when they are scheduled to attend next.
- Ex-members – raise awareness that we dropped the ball and discuss what we could have done better.

To keep your school efficient, you should have clear start and finish times, along with an agenda. Do not let the team take over the meeting; you need to keep it on point. I also used to hold a tracking chart for team members and analyse who was late, who contributed the most, who was the most positive (and the most negative), and who had the best attitude. I wanted to build a killer team, not a collection of people who didn't care.

In summary, holding team meetings is not a waste of time; it's an investment into your business. Meetings can be a great way to improve your team and ensure everybody is pulling the same way.

Chapter 16

Hold Weekly Team Training

I always did this immediately after the weekly meeting. Monday afternoon, from 12 to 2 pm, was our weekly meeting and weekly team training. I found that doing it at the start of the week set the tone and direction for the week. The team training was a rotation every week for eight weeks (a typical grading cycle) to cover the major functions of the business. The more your team is trained, the better they will perform. We used to cover:

- Initial call
- Confirmation call
- Meet and greet 1
- Meet and greet 2
- Consultation delivery
- Enrolment conference
- Attendance calls
- Plus more

Holding weekly team training will only improve your school's professionalism. The more you practice, the better your desired outcomes will be, meaning the more successful your school will be. We have all been somewhere and had a great experience, only to return and have a completely different experience because the person who dealt with you before was not there. You want your students and parents to have an excellent, consistent experience every time. The more professional you are, the more it ties into your uniqueness.

In summary, team training is a high-value task. You are passing on your knowledge and steering your team to carry out the desired behaviours. Don't underestimate how crucial team training is to growing a professional school.

Chapter 17

Have A Timetable
That Will Allow You To Grow

Do not have an 'all grades, all ages' timetable that allows people to train at 6 pm or 7 pm. Yes, I did this for years, thinking that giving my parents options was better. Your students need to be given the opportunity to train every day you are open, but it's not a choice between the 6 pm one, the 7 pm one, or the 8 pm one. When you give them the choice, you will notice that less important things push you to the side, i.e. football training. I'm not saying football training is not important, but what I am saying is that it doesn't develop a skillset of truly transferable LIFE SKILLS that will help them throughout the rest of their lives.

You need to separate your classes so that parents can see there is a different level: trial enrolment, Black Belt Training, and Master & Leadership. If you are just starting off, then it may be hard to do this, but the more you concentrate on marketing and the more members you get, the more you will need the separation of your classes/programmes. Please do not have a one-size-fits-all class timetable. I believe I am a good instructor, as I am sure you are. I believe I could differentiate and challenge my students according to their grade and experience. However, separating your timetable into specific levels helps retention and improves student standard.

If you only have a small following and no senior/advanced grades, then don't feel you need to have an equal number of classes for each grade. You shouldn't have a timetable that reflects an active count of 300 students if you only have 20-50 students. Your school should have lots of intro slots, lots of trial enrolment classes, and then maybe one higher-level class.

Dervish Dervish

Chapter 18

Maintain Good Cash Flow

When you start to market your school and have a clear enrolment process, you will begin to see your monthly tuition grow – great! This, in turn, means your cash flow should also be increasing if you manage to achieve a positive net enrolment each month.

Do not let your lifestyle grow with your tuition. By that, I mean do not let your expenses grow along with your income. The number of instructors I speak to who say they 'have' to get something now that they've enrolled more members is alarming. You want to keep your expenses as low as possible. The only things you should be spending money on are:

- Your rent
- Your staff
- Marketing (should be 20% of your gross)
- Communications (internet, phone, etc.)
- Equipment

There will, of course, be other items that you need to purchase, such as stock and cleaning items, but the above should be the biggest part of your expenses.

Have all your tuition paid on the 1st of the month. Do not let tuition stagger at various stages of the month because you feel it will help your members. Have all your expenses paid on the 15th of the month. Other money coming in outside of those dates should be initial investments, tuition paid before the first payment, renewal top-ups, etc. On the 16th of the month, you want to have a very good idea of how much cash you have until the next tuition payment is made on the 1st of the month.

All great business owners pay themselves first; therefore, on the 15th of the month, I would set up to pay yourself. If this then turns your cash flow upside down, it will be an incentive for you to increase marketing and enrol/renew more students. If you wait to see how much money is left at the end of the month, it's very easy for you not to be paid. Nobody would work as hard as you do all month for free, so why should you? Remember that you are building a business and not working for free. I want you to build a successful business, not just 'own a job.'

I was lucky enough to have great cash flow for many years. If you've always had it, you don't really appreciate it until it goes. I remember my accountant each year saying, 'Your cash flow is great.' I didn't really understand why he had to say that because I thought all businesses were like that. That is how I want all my mentees to feel – I want them to have great cash-flowing businesses.

Other elements I have not covered but you should be tracking include:

- % of your active count that graded
- Lifetime value of your students
- Average student value per calendar month
- When retention calls are being carried out (and by whom)
- What marketing is being carried out this week (and by whom)
- Plus much more

Like all elements of this book, there are many more things I can cover, and I can go into much more detail about the finer aspects of running a school. I suggest you read this book at least twice. Get in touch with me if you want help or to work with me to really grow your school so that it becomes the most professional school around.

Chapter 19

Importance Of Tracking, Measuring, & Tweaking Your Stats

I am so surprised at the number of instructors I speak to, who say things like, "We're just not doing as much business as we used to," or, "Our sales are down," or, "Our lessons are excellent, but we can't sign people up." These are good things to realise, but you need to know exactly where the holes in your system are so you can improve that part of your business. Professional sports teams watch their recent games and analyse the good and bad. They then put strategies in place to maintain the good and improve the bad. You need to have that mindset with your school. I was continually giving team members feedback (probably too much in hindsight). Our school was called 'Kaizen-Do,' so I was insistent on continually improving every element of our operation.

I explain it this way to my mentees: if you ever have to go to hospital, one of the first things they do is triage you. As part of that procedure, they often take your blood pressure and oxygen levels. There are, of course, more things they measure, as well as asking your age. They do that so they can group or bundle you into a certain set of data and then have an idea of where to start your treatment (or where to place you in the emergency queue). If you don't know your stats, then you really don't know your business at all. Don't worry though – this book will help you with that.

You Must Know Your Stats

As a business owner, it is essential that you know your key stats. The head instructor at my school used to have to email me the stats for that day at the end of every single day. The stats were also uploaded to a Google Drive spreadsheet that I could view in further detail. The stats were then compared to our monthly Key Result Areas (KRAs). If things started to slip, we had procedures in place to get things back on track. Other than during the months following March 20th, 2020 (Covid), when business suffered, our stats never fell off the edge of a cliff. I used to analyse them with a microscope to prevent anything from getting too bad.

How did we do during Covid? We still enrolled people virtually until the lockdowns were lifted. It's not all negative though. When you start to take more money and enrol more members, you can see how your business is growing by looking at the same stats.

The first level of key stats you need to track every day is:

- Number of enquiries
- Number of first lessons (aka intros/consultations)
- Number of second lessons
- Number of enrolment conferences (ECs)
- Number of enrolments
- Money taken
- Ex-members
- Net enrolment this month

The next level on top of that would include:

- Number of renewal conferences (RCs)
- Number of renewals
- Percentage of enrolment conferences to enrolments
- Percentage of renewal conferences to renewals
- N.B. Name(s) and address(es) of any new enrolments and new renewals were also included, so I could personally write them a welcome letter. I wanted the welcome letter to arrive within 24 hours of enrolment

(you need to avoid buyer's remorse and it's a great positive touch point).

A higher level than that would also include:

- Percentage of enquiries to percentage of booked first lessons
- Percentage of booked first lessons to percentage of attended first lessons
- Percentage of first lessons that then attended second lessons
- Percentage of first lesson students that came back for a second lesson and were graded 'A'
- Percentage of second lesson 'A' students who had an EC

Lifetime value of a student and revenue per student are also great metrics to track. For example, having a school with a 300 active count sounds good, but if the LTV is only £200, it's very bad compared to an active count of 75 with an LTV of £2000. I often explain to my mentees that it's not how big your school is; it's dependent on your LTV. What's the point in having 500 students if they are only paying you £20pcm, compared to 100 students paying you £200pcm?

The above then forms the basis for your spreadsheet.

I could write a separate book on stats because I needed to track and measure every element of the business. You could be grossing a large amount of money. For some clubs, that might be £1000–£2000pcm; for others, it might be £5000–£10,000pcm. For us, we were regularly doing £25,000–£30,000pcm (I was running my other business at this point) and I wanted to know where the slippage was taking place. As a business owner, you need to fill all the holes in your bucket. If I had not wanted to expand my property portfolio, I could have comfortably built the gross up to £50,000pcm, £60,000pcm, or even £83,333pcm in tuition alone (not including primary school work and private lessons). One of my great property mentors, who is a very successful man, suggested I write this book so I could help the next breed of instructors improve their operations and, as a result, the Martial Arts organisations. So, if you are enjoying this book and finding a lot of value, then it was my property mentor who laid the seed (we all need mentors).

If you are not tracking your stats daily, then you need to start if you want to run a successful business. If you don't want to create a spreadsheet, then just put the first level of stats above on a clipboard so they can be recorded for the week. You can then look at it at the end of the month to see where your strengths and weaknesses are. On a side note, the number 1 in your business is always bad: one key instructor, one key contract, one key source of marketing, etc. The number 1 in your business is too risky.

What Gets Measured Gets Done

I think it was Peter Drucker who once said, "What gets measured gets done." What I took from that was that if we were going through a dry couple of days with enquiries, we would ramp up the marketing. The simple reason being that whatever we were doing at that moment was not working as it should be (that is why you should NEVER rely on just 1-3 marketing sources). You need multiple levels of continuous marketing going on.

Don't Make It Sound Better Than It Is

At no point should you or your team count an enrolment if they have not finalised every part of the payment, i.e., paid their initial and set up their agreement for tuition. One of our team sayings was, "Don't make it sound better than it actually is." For instance, if a family is fantastic and gave all the buying signals but did not actually pay everything they needed to because they have to go and think about it, then do not count that as an enrolment. That is counted as a failed EC. Only count them as an enrolment if they have paid what they need to pay and crossed the T's and dotted the I's.

End of Month Report

The daily stats then form the monthly stats, which is where your 'end of month report' should come in. I would be passed the detailed EOM report by the 1st or 2nd of the month and it would form the basis of the EOM training. This was when we had a large team meeting and addressed the things we needed to work on, such as:

- Was it that we didn't have enough enquiries?
- Was it that we were struggling to get them to the first lesson?
- Was it that they were coming to the second lesson unprepared?
- Was one instructor getting a better first-to-second attendance percentage than another one? If one Sensei continually got the best percentage of students to return for a second lesson, then we would record their intros/consultations and analyse what they were doing that other instructors weren't.
- Were students not renewing to Black Belt by the 8th week? If not, then why not?
- What was wrong with our orientation process? Did they have two progress folder conferences, regular progress checks, frequent calls, positive touchpoints, etc.?

You probably get the impression now that I was quite a tyrant when it came to team training, and I was, because this was my business and I wanted to make it a success. One of the worst things you can do is do hardly any training and then expect your school to run well when you're not there; it doesn't happen. Just like your sparring, basic techniques, katas, and pad work, they need continual practice. Don't expect to train somebody once and then for them to have perfected it. You know yourself, it doesn't work that way. I remember the times when staff training had slipped and then, when you role-play, it was clear that important things had been missed and bad habits had crept in.

In summary, I hope this section hasn't daunted you. It's just like a competition: how do you know who is winning if you're not keeping score? Even if you are winning, how can you improve your performance? How can you make things more efficient? My school is called Kaizen-Do Karate. 'Kaizen-Do' means 'the way of continual improvement,' and that concept is EXACTLY what you want your school and your instructors to embed. It's not that you are never happy; it's more about you knowing you can do better.

Part 4

IT'S A BUSINESS, A DEEPER LOOK

Chapter 20

Goal Setting is a Major Component of Your Retention

Going back to the first chapter in this book, your number one goal is to enrol a student and keep them forever. You can have lots of marketing in place and enrol 10, 20, or even 30 students a month, but if you are not retaining them, it's a pointless exercise. I would rather grow by +2 students a month—which means I have gained +24 students by the end of the year—than enrol 20 a month and lose 22, meaning I have shrunk by 24 students at the end of the year. It all comes down to your monthly net enrolment, and this is a stat you MUST track every single month.

I want my mentees to comfortably enrol +10 students every month and maintain a net enrolment of +8. Before I became serious and meticulous about tracking stats, I only tracked the number of enrolments and would guess how many students we lost—this is ludicrous. Only tracking your enrolments is like only looking at your salary without considering your expenses; before you know it, you will be in financial trouble. It's like tracking the number of goals you've scored without considering how many you've conceded. It's no coincidence that the more obsessive I became about tracking statistics, the better the school became. If you want to build and run a successful school, you must track your stats daily. It is your job to market your school and plug the holes in your retention.

Master of Retention

You need to be a master of retention and familiar with various retention strategies. Look after the student first and their technical skills second. Just like marketing, there is no single tool that will solve all your retention problems. I am often asked, "How do you keep so many of your students?" This usually happens after someone visits my school and sees strong student numbers across all grades. It wasn't structured like a pyramid—with a wide base of white belts gradually narrowing until only one Black Belt remained at the top. Based on my extensive experience, some retention strategies are more effective than others, but all contribute to overall success.

Setting a Goal to Black Belt Improves Retention

The number one retention tool is your ability to help students set the goal of becoming a Black Belt. This is a crucial part of running your school and will significantly impact both your students' success and your business's profitability. However, let's not forget that everything we do is to help students stay committed and reap the lifelong benefits of Black Belt training. Yes, you deserve to be paid for your work, but it's ultimately about your students gaining the same benefits you have experienced on your own journey.

You must educate parents on why training for a Black Belt with you is a valuable part of their child's educational development. If they view your classes as "just something to do" or categorise them as a recreational sport, they will likely drop out at the first sign of boredom. Parents must genuinely appreciate the significance of earning a Black Belt.

If you are reading this, you have likely been involved in martial arts for at least five years—some of you for 10, 15, or even 20 years, and some perhaps even longer than my 30 years. What you need to help your new students understand is the endless transferable benefits of a Black Belt journey. I'm not just talking about physical skills; it's about the entire developmental process. I am not just a 6th-degree Black Belt—it is a major part of who I am. There is no way I would have achieved what I have in life without the skills martial arts have instilled in me. I expect the same is true for you.

These skills include the ability to resist peer pressure, the discipline to set, work towards, and achieve goals, and the determination to persevere. It took self-control to maintain a healthy diet during my peak fitness, resilience to work 120-hour weeks across three jobs (which landed me in intensive care—but that's a story for another time), and financial discipline to support myself through university without debt. In fact, I was the only student in my third year driving a Mercedes—I must have looked like a complete idiot! That was before I truly understood assets and liabilities, passive income, or how to leverage my time and resources.

As a side note, one of my other businesses is a property coaching mentorship, and I've found many principles overlap between building a property portfolio and running a martial arts school. As your school grows, you may want to allocate some of your profits to property investment.

Goals+Commitment = Success: A Higher-Level Programme

You need to structure your programmes carefully—some students will have committed to earning their Black Belt, while others will be on a trial enrolment programme. As I mentioned earlier, you should not have a timetable that accommodates "all ages, all abilities, all grades" in a single session.

When I first implemented this in 2016, I struggled to wrap my head around it. I was completely set in my ways, as I'm sure many of you reading this are. I was raised in an environment where every grade was taught together, following the same curriculum. You didn't "commit" to earning a Black Belt—you either dropped out along the way, or you kept training until you achieved 1st degree and then dropped out.

Ask yourself this: were you one of the few who stayed or one of the many who quit? I can guarantee you were one of the few. I can also guarantee that if my karate school were assessed on its graduation rate—the percentage of white belts who made it to Black Belt—it would have been around 0.5%. That means for every 200 white belts who enrolled, only one would reach Black Belt. If I had been running a primary or secondary school, I would have been condemned for such poor graduation rates.

Why do we allow this to happen? Imagine all the amazing Black Belts we could have developed if only they had stuck with it a little longer—if they had been nurtured just a bit more. Their lives could have changed for the better, just as yours did. We didn't try hard enough to get them to commit to the Black Belt journey. We didn't make it clear what they were missing by not earning that Black Belt.

Compare this to how parents value a university degree. I have a degree and a PGCE, but I never really aspired to earn them or become a lecturer—I just fell into it. I felt obliged to go to university because my parents followed the traditional mindset: "Go to school, go to college, go to university, get a degree, then get a good job." I now realise that this is an outdated, Victorian way of thinking.

Of course, if my children want to go to university, they are free to do so, but there are many paths to success. As the great Jim Rohn said, "Formal education will make you a living; self-education will make you a fortune." The more you educate yourself in your chosen field, the more you will stand out, and the greater your rewards will be.

Explain All the Skills a Black Belt Journey Has to Offer Their Child

It's your job as an instructor and professional business owner to clearly demonstrate how critical training to Black Belt with you at your unique school is. At the time of writing this, all three of my children are Black Belts. I'm not trying to relive my youth through them, but I do want them to acquire the transferable LIFE SKILLS that the Black Belt journey—and beyond—has to offer.

I want them to develop focus, respect, discipline, grit, determination, perseverance, self-control, resilience, modesty, humility, and self-discipline. You get the idea.

Getting students and parents to understand the value of training to Black Belt starts from their first introductory lesson. Once they enrol, they are educated over the next eight weeks on the importance of committing to Black Belt. They receive emails, links to testimonials, and direct mail, all of which help them commit to becoming a Black Belt.

I will explain this in more detail later, but the main thing you need to understand is that to retain more students, they need to set the goal of becoming a Black Belt. Character tabs, self-discipline medals, self-discipline trophies (earned through completion of self-discipline sheets), visualisation posters, plus holding goal-setting sessions twice a year, all help parents understand that training to Black Belt and beyond is essential—and that it's what students at your school do.

In summary, if you want your students to stay with you for longer, then you need to convince (not hoodwink) them that committing to and training to Black Belt and beyond with you is just as important as obtaining their GCSEs. You must clearly demonstrate how a journey to Black Belt at your school will contribute to their child's development.

Chapter 21

The Renewal Process & Why You NEED To Renew Students

The Importance of Renewing Students

Just as important as constantly marketing your school is your role in renewing students after they have enrolled. Renewing students ensures they receive the full benefits of a Black Belt journey while also improving your retention and monthly revenue. Renewing students should be a win-win outcome. The following paragraphs will clarify why you need to fully understand the renewal process and how it can catapult your growth.

Minimal Growth Before I Started Renewing Students

For the first 14 years of running my school, I did not renew any of my students. My school steadily grew by a few percent each year. In hindsight, my growth was only slightly ahead of inflation, so I didn't perform as well as I had thought. The cost of belts and suits was rising, but my prices didn't keep up because I was afraid of being too expensive.

I didn't believe my programme or my teaching was any more valuable than someone who was just teaching kicks and punches once or twice per week. However, as soon as I started renewing students, my school's gross income jumped from hovering around £9,000 per month in tuition to £15,000, then £18,000, and eventually £24,000.

Not renewing your students is business suicide. That said, like all things in this book, you must approach it with the students' best interests at heart. You should only renew students you genuinely want to work with moving forward.

The Trial Enrolment Programme

Every student who joins your school enrols on a trial programme. This programme is designed to introduce them to the basics of your teaching and help them decide if they want to commit to becoming a Black Belt. At the same time, it allows us to assess whether we want to work with them through their Black Belt journey and beyond.

It is a foundation programme—it introduces students to the benefits of your school, but it is not meant to make them the best yellow or orange belts you've ever had. I lost hundreds of brilliant students at the yellow belt stage simply because I tightened the screw too soon. The training intensity increased too quickly—from a manageable white belt syllabus to a yellow belt syllabus that suddenly required free sparring.

I lost so many students because of bad practice. Instead of building Black Belts, I was filtering out those who didn't want to work hard. What I should have done was develop their mindset and perseverance gradually at each belt level.

Imagine if I had truly committed them to becoming Black Belts and helped their parents envision their child as a Black Belt with all these transferable LIFE SKILLS. Do you think I would have had fewer dropouts and a more successful school?

Demonstrating the Value of a Black Belt

Explaining every element of the renewal process would be difficult, but the key to success is your ability to demonstrate how becoming a Black Belt will improve a child's life.

When I first introduced this concept to my team, I used the university example. Most parents want their child to go to university. But going to university doesn't necessarily mean someone is cleverer than others or guaranteed a successful career. What it does provide is a qualification that demonstrates knowledge in a certain area and, to some extent, a level of discipline and commitment.

You need to show parents that training at your school to Black Belt and beyond will open doors for their child in the future. A true Black Belt journey should be much more than just learning how to kick someone in the chin. Your students will develop:

- The ability to resist negative peer pressure
- The ability to set and achieve goals
- The mindset to keep trying
- A commitment to self-improvement

They will also see improvements in:

- Discipline
- Determination
- Perseverance
- Self-control

- Respect
- Resilience
- Humility
- Grit
- Drive
- Etiquette

Linking It to an Academic Achievement Parents Recognise

At our school, training to 1st Degree Black Belt was equivalent to gaining GCSEs. Training to 2nd Degree Black Belt was like gaining A-levels, and 3rd Degree was comparable to earning a university degree.

Now, I'm not saying that our Black Belt ranks are recognised as official academic qualifications. However, we wanted parents to understand that the longer their child trains, the more they will benefit.

Most parents want their child to achieve GCSEs because they recognise the standard of education associated with them. It was our job to ensure parents viewed earning a Black Belt at our school as an equally valuable achievement in their child's personal development.

Commitment Is the Key

Everyone at your school who interacts with students must be able to clearly explain why committing to Black Belt training will help them in many areas of their lives.

If you want to build a great business, the days of simply signing up students (bad terminology) and hoping they stick around are over. How has that approach worked for you so far?

Students need to commit to becoming a Black Belt. Like any life decision, if you don't make a decision, you have—by default—decided not to do anything.

The same applies to Black Belt training. If students don't commit, they are highly unlikely to achieve it.

Goals + Commitment = Success.

When Do You Renew Them?

The simple answer is: when they are ready. You do not try to renew a student if they are not ready. Some signs that they are not ready to renew include:

- If they do not attend two lessons a week regularly.

- If only one parent is turning up to lessons.

- If they are not earning lots of character stripes and medals (this is a big one).

- If they are not completing visualisation posters or goal-setting sheets.

- If they are 'B' parents.

You do not wait until the end of the 12-month trial enrolment programme. If you do, you will have lost all the beginner's momentum. Waiting too long to renew means that by the time you attempt to do so, many students will have already dropped out. Ultimately, the longer you leave it, the smaller your pool of students available for renewal becomes. If the parents' goals align with your Black Belt training outcomes, then you owe it to them to renew their child's commitment to Black Belt training.

The Goldilocks Zone

The absolute ideal time to renew them is as soon after enrolment as possible. However, there is a 'Goldilocks Zone'—the timing has to be just right. You cannot expect to renew a student in their third-ever lesson at your school (their first lesson as an official student).

We had an orientation process that started as soon as a student enrolled. This process involved physical mail, emails, regular communication in class and over the phone, but the most important part was building rapport with parents. Do not come across as the high-and-mighty master martial arts instructor. Instead, speak to them in a way that highlights how being a Black Belt has massively helped you in your own life (which I'm sure it has).

I genuinely believe that I would not have earned my degree, completed a PGCE, built up a successful karate school, or developed a property portfolio if it weren't for the priceless skills that martial arts have taught me.

Having regular progress checks, holding the progress folder conference, and sending information and testimonials about Black Belt training all contribute to the renewal process. We had normally convinced parents at around the six-week mark (10–12 lessons) that committing to Black Belt was a great investment in their child's future.

Please note what I said there: it's an *investment*. Like any good investment, it will reap benefits later down the line, and you will be glad you made it (sorry, a bit of my property business mindset coming through there). Each of your team members needs to 100% agree that training to Black Belt is a crucial part of every student's development.

For any student who, for some reason, has not renewed within a reasonable timeframe (less than 2.5 months), you have the opportunity to renew them during your *Goal-Setting Season*. Following strict advice from my mentor, we held this twice a year in the month leading up to our Black Belt gradings. This allowed us to pick up any students who had not yet renewed while also re-engaging those who had already committed.

In summary, I will say it again: if you do not have a renewal process at your school, you are losing far too many students, and you are doing a disservice to their parents. You are leaving money on the table and not making your school as profitable as it could be.

Your job as a professional is to be paid properly for the service you provide. Your job as a business owner is to make your business as successful as you want it to be.

Chapter 22

Always Be Marketing

Having an active count of over 300 students was the result of tried-and-tested marketing. Regardless of how good our guestology or student standards were, that meant nothing if we couldn't get people through the door.

One of my mentors once said that after this book, I should write one solely on marketing for new students. I'm not saying that to brag—I'm saying it to give you an idea of how extensive this section could have been. Over 20 years, I have tried hundreds of different marketing strategies and spent probably £50,000–£75,000 attracting students to my school. As you would expect, some worked better than others.

Marketing Is a System, Not a One-Off Event

The success of your school's growth depends heavily on the continuity and effectiveness of your marketing. To maintain a steady stream of new students, you need to market your school constantly. Never stop marketing. Any business that stops marketing inevitably starts to decline. The decline may not be noticeable at first, but trust me, it's happening.

If you have read any sales books, you will have come across the ABC principle: *Always Be Closing*. ABC means you need to ask for the sale, present a clear price, and then assume the customer will buy. For a martial arts business owner like you, this means clearly stating the price of tuition and the initial investment, then assuming the student will enrol.

If you want to run a successful business, you need to adopt the *ABM* mindset: *Always Be Marketing.*

Marketing Spend Should Be the Last Thing You Cut

Never, ever cut back on your marketing—this is what feeds new students into your school. If you ever think, *I'm going to stop advertising because we're doing okay*, trust me, from experience, that is the worst thing you can do.

During COVID, we immediately pivoted our online lead generation to virtual lessons. We managed to enrol about 12 students in a three-month period—not great, and nothing compared to our normal three-month enrolment rate, but it kept a flow of white belts coming in. At the time, we were spending about £1,500 per month on internet advertising alone. That may sound like a lot to you right now, but as your school grows, your marketing budget should grow too. Each month, you should allocate a percentage of your gross income to marketing—never be tight on reinvestment into your business.

After speaking to many sports club businesses and martial arts school owners, it is clear that 99% do little to no marketing. I frequently speak to Senseis who say things like, *Well, we could do this... or we could do that...*, usually followed by, *When I get some time, I'll design some leaflets and drop a few off at some shops nearby.*

Designing and printing a few leaflets to put in local shops is not going to create a steady flow of new white belts. Trust me, I know—I've done it.

If you are currently doing zero marketing and your membership base is "okay," imagine what a well-planned and implemented marketing strategy could do for your student count and your monthly revenue. This is one of the first items I help my mentees with. Remember, when we use the word *okay*, it's often interchangeable with *so-so*. If you were truly happy with your *so-so* school, you wouldn't have invested in this book or taken the time to read it.

2004: No Marketing = No Profits

When I first started back in 2004, I had no marketing plan, nor did I bother to educate myself on the subject. My "marketing" consisted of printing off some posters I had designed on my computer—using some rubbish clip-art karate figure—and sticking them in about 10 local shops.

I was cheap.

If a shop charged me something small, like 50p a week, I would scoff and say, *Okay, here's £3—please keep my advert up for six weeks.* That was my penny-pinching, scarcity mentality.

After all, I was a Black Belt 2nd Dan, an excellent instructor (in my mind), and studying sports science at university—people were *bound* to come flocking.

How wrong I was.

Track and Understand Your ROI

One principle you need to understand is ROI: *Return on Investment.*

For those of you who follow my property business, you'll know that I always look at ROI alongside other key metrics. For my property company, our number one metric is *ROCE*—Return on Capital Employed. I want to know exactly how hard our invested money is working and how much profit it is generating.

When running your martial arts school, you need to track how much you spend on marketing, how many leads and enquiries you receive, how many first and second lessons are attended, and ultimately, how many students enrol.

Once you know how much you spend on marketing and how many students you enrol, you can calculate your ROI.

Our ROI varied from as little as £200 to over £2,000 per student. On average, it worked out at about £325 per enrolment. Some school owners might look at that figure and think it's expensive, but when you know the *Lifetime Value* (LTV) of your students, you realise that by month two, the money is recouped—and everything after that is profit.

When we secured students for £200, it was because we were running a lot of marketing and successfully closing a high number of enrolments. When the cost shot up to £2,000 per student, it was usually because we weren't getting enough enquiries booked in, our intro lessons were weak, the second lesson experience was poor, or our enrolment process wasn't effective.

As you learn more about running your school, you will see that *nothing* stands alone—everything affects everything else.

My Biggest Mistake: Not Educating Myself

My biggest mistake in those early days was not educating myself properly. You *must* invest in your own learning. Mentors speed up your journey and help you avoid costly mistakes.

Think back to your martial arts training. Did you achieve your high grade just by watching YouTube videos? I highly doubt it. You were taught by a higher grade—someone more experienced and knowledgeable in the art.

The same principle applies to marketing and every other aspect of your business. Learn from someone who has walked the path before you and achieved what you aspire to achieve.

Yes, I mentor many people, but I still invest in mentors myself—because I know I have even more potential to unlock.

Different Types of Marketing

If you have read marketing books before, then you will understand that to be effective, you need to have multiple types of marketing running simultaneously. If you have read any of Jay Abraham's books on marketing, he refers to it as a *Parthenon of marketing*, meaning that you need many pillars holding up your business.

I had read this over and over again but never implemented it—until I had a mentor who basically put a foot up my backside and said, *"Get more marketing done."* My mentor held me accountable, and it helped me grow my school.

When I started reading marketing books, I tried to implement what I could. However, I now realise that much of the marketing I was doing was what the big companies, like Coca-Cola, do—I was brand advertising (another mistake). As a small business, this is one of the worst things you can do. You end up spending hundreds, or in my case, thousands of pounds just to get your logo out there—what a waste.

Yes, you do need to be everywhere at all times. Being omnipresent is good, but your marketing needs to be as targeted as possible and working. The smaller your business, the more focused you need to be. A great mentor of mine once said, *"You need to go narrow and deep."*

For example, if your ideal student is a boy or girl between six and seven years old, then advertise wherever their parents are likely to see it. Here in the UK, 99% of our ideal students attend primary school. As soon as we started advertising in primary schools, we began to see real results.

I have marketed to primary schools for over ten years and often use a multi-pronged approach, such as:

- Sending a letter

- Following up with an information pack

- Sending an email

- Making a phone call

- Sending another pack of information

- Visiting in person

Never expect to send *one* letter and be bombarded with enquiries.

The same principle applies to marketing your school—don't assume that sending out 10,000 leaflets will flood your school with students. You need to have multiple marketing strategies running each and every month.

Marketing We Used

Some of the strategies I have tried over the years worked better than others. In no particular order, here are some things I have done:

- Facebook ads

- SEO (Search Engine Optimisation)

- Advertising on black cab taxis (had nine at one point)

- Advertising on regular taxis (had 15+ at one point)

- 12ft × 6ft billboards (had six at one point)

- Advertising at our local football club

- Mass leaflet drops using a local distribution company

- Delivering leaflets directly to primary schools (one per child)

- Attending *loads* of events, such as:

    o   Winter and summer fairs

    o   Garden centre open days

    o   Bag-packing at supermarkets

    o   Charity days

    o   Plus many more I've forgotten!

- Placing flags at the bottom of our street to raise awareness of our school

- Placing 2.5ft × 2ft *Correx* signs near our school

- Advertising in local shops (post offices, newsagents, cafés, etc.)

- Leaving A5 leaflet holders in *hundreds* of shops across our town

- Holding classes in a park on nice sunny days

All of the above are external marketing methods, which have the most impact. However, I hardly did any internal marketing (another mistake). When I had an active student count of over 150, I *should* have layered in internal marketing to encourage my existing members to regularly refer new students.

Other Key Marketing Strategies

Learning more about marketing helped my school grow. As with all things in business, some strategies work better than others. This is not an exhaustive list, but here are some key things you should be doing to increase student enrolment:

- Signs outside your school

- Signs inside your school

- Leaflet drops to *every* primary school within a three-mile radius of your school (then expand to 4–5 miles, then 6–7 miles, etc.)

- Organising a *free* day of taster lessons at primary schools (there's a crucial component to this, which I'll discuss later)

- Delivering *free* taster lessons at Boy Scout and Girl Guide groups

- Delivering *free* taster lessons at nurseries (this builds awareness among parents for when their child is old enough, plus many children have older siblings)

- Getting featured in your local free online newspaper or magazine with an article about you and the benefits of training at *your* unique school

- Texting, emailing, and sending letters to your existing students, inviting them to a *Buddy Day*

- Organising themed parties—St Patrick's Day, Summer, Halloween, Christmas, etc.

- Facebook ads

- Google SEO

- Attending local events where parents and children are likely to be present

Even if you run your business from a part-time venue, you can still implement many of the above strategies.

Just Start

Don't be overwhelmed. I can help with your marketing plan, and can help you gain +20 new members each month (if you decide to work with me) but what you need to do is just plan the next 30 days.

If you've never done any systemised marketing before, planning and executing a 30-day strategy will significantly boost your enquiries and enrolments. Just aim to do one thing—no matter how small—to attract attention to your school.

Once you complete those initial 30 days, you can then plan the next 90 days. Repeat some of the things that worked in the first 30 days and add additional marketing tasks.

The goal is to *start*. Don't procrastinate. And yes, I may have said this before, but:

Action = Results.

It's often said that *"Knowledge is power,"* but I believe it should be:

"Applied knowledge is power."

Implement the strategies from this book if you want your business to be successful.

Keep Your Special Offer Consistent

Your special offer should always be the same, regardless of where someone sees your marketing or which leaflet they pick up. Everyone should qualify for a two-week free pass.

Do not create separate offers for different marketing campaigns— just keep it simple and consistent.

At one point, we foolishly ran 30-day free passes, but these had a terrible conversion rate. If I were to implement them again, I would structure them differently, ensuring they followed the same enrolment process as all other leads. Back then, we allowed people to attend for 29 days before trying to sell to them—please do not do this. We learned the hard way that we were just being busy fools.

I don't claim to be the fountain of knowledge, but I am honest about the mistakes that prevented us from growing. At the back of this book, I've compiled a list of mistakes. However, that list could easily have been 500+ mistakes I've made!

AIDA – The Key to Effective Marketing

The primary objective of any marketing strategy is to get their attention—that's it!

Marketing books often refer to the AIDA principle:

- **Attention** – Grab their attention with a strong headline (*not* your logo).

- **Interest** – Spark their interest—make them think, *"That's interesting."*

- **Desire** – Create desire—make them *want* what you're offering.

- **Action** – Get them to *act now* by contacting you immediately.

If you successfully capture their attention and they respond to your Call to Action (CTA), then it's down to you and your systems to bring them through your front door.

You are *not* trying to enrol them at the leaflet stage—you're simply trying to grab their attention and get them to contact you.

Getting people through your front door is the hardest part. Once they're in, it's up to *you* to make sure they stay.

You're a Professional, Not Just a Coach

I have visited probably over 100 primary schools within a 6-mile radius of my karate school. I wanted people to know about Kaizen-Do Karate and Sensei Dervish's unique character development programme. When you do visit primary schools, however, you must position yourself properly. You are NOT just a local martial arts instructor with a Black Belt. You are a professional. You're not someone who has a full-time job and does this on the side for a bit of extra money. If you do have a full-time job, keep this to yourself – they don't need to know that information. You need to position yourself, but more importantly, your programme, as highly valuable and a clear educational tool that will complement any child's formal education. Doing this is more of an art than a science, which I am not going to go into here.

Your marketing needs to be consistent. If you only do 2-3 things a month, then do those every month. Don't do 20 things in one month, enrol a few students, and then do nothing for a year. You need to be consistent with your marketing. I used to carry out team training so that when enquiries contacted us, we could ask, "So, how did you find out about us?" When our marketing was consistent for many years, we often got the reply, "Are you kidding? You guys are everywhere!" When we heard that response, we knew we were doing a good job. We wanted to occupy a section in everyone's mind. We wanted people who hadn't even been to our school to be able to recommend us to anyone who asked about karate.

When you start marketing and layer on more and more over time, I guarantee there will be a point where you are getting more white belts than you ever thought possible. When this 'champagne problem' happens, do not stop marketing. You may face the 'champagne problem' of your classes getting too full, or you might question the size of your venue. If so, then good – these are great problems to have. I enjoy helping my mentees with those problems. Do not get a bigger venue, do not hire carelessly, and, whatever you do, don't stop marketing. Most of your 'champagne problems' can be solved by designing your timetable correctly. You should be tracking class sizes and working out which are your busier and quieter days. You can then add classes accordingly. However, do not stop or reduce your marketing.

Planning and implementing your marketing are the major pieces of the marketing puzzle, but you must then assess its effectiveness. In other words, you need to record how successful the marketing was. At one event, we gained about 10 leads. I sent a team member there for about five hours. It was in a very bad area of our town, and I was in two minds whether to cancel the event (I didn't actually book it – the team member in charge did, so they could reach their KPI). Gathering 10 leads in 5 hours is terrible. However, from those 10 leads, just two showed up at our school (already a poor 20% show rate), but one of them became our highest-paying member. Paying a team member to go to an event for 5 hours just to get 2 more intro students is not ideal. However, that event brought in a member who was paying £349 per month. I'm not advocating that you attend events in lower demographic areas of your town, but it shows that every now and then, it can work out in your favour.

Marketing I Have Not Discussed

As I mentioned earlier, I didn't want to turn this into a huge section and cause overwhelm. This book was created to help school owners improve, and I do hope it does that. Some other marketing strategies you should consider include:

- **Social media**: I was admittedly well behind the curve on this. I should have gotten past my dislike of social media and utilised it more to enhance my business. Don't make the same mistake. Utilise Facebook Reels and TikTok videos. Encourage parents to tag your school on their posts. Use all social media as a business tool.

- **Blogs**: These are great for your website so that when parents look there, they can see you are not just a 'physical' instructor. Blogs should focus on the benefits of your tuition, such as improved focus, respect, discipline, determination, etc.

- **YouTube**: Set up a YouTube channel. Of course, create the usual physical videos, but also make videos based on your blog articles. Your prospective parents won't really want to watch you doing your favourite moves, but they will be interested in you explaining how your programme improves character.

All the Team Needs to Market Your School

The main point I want you to take from this chapter is that to get students, you need to market for them. Every team member needs to understand that they have a role in marketing and promoting your school. Your instructors do not only teach. There is no magic pill – you need to market constantly. One of our team's sayings was, "Action = Results." This definitely applies to your marketing. Don't complain about not having any new students if you're not doing any advertising. How are people supposed to know about you if you don't tell them? Complaining about not having enough new students without doing any marketing is like complaining that you are overweight but not training enough and having a bad diet. You don't wait until the 27th, 28th, 29th, or 30th of the month to complain about a bad month. You know by the end of week one if you're on track or not. If you're behind by the end of week one and week two, then you need to do more marketing and train more on creating value on the floor.

In summary, start marketing your school, enrol members, and you will notice an increase in your active count and monthly gross. Everything leads back to your marketing; without it, your school stagnates and ultimately dies.

Chapter 23

Guestology Engineer Every Part of Your Family's Experience

This is such an important element of your school. Have you ever been somewhere where nobody greeted you, nobody made eye contact, and you just felt unwelcome or that you were interrupting their day? That is the exact opposite of what you want your school to be like.

You need your school to be a friendly and welcoming place with a great atmosphere. For any of you old enough to remember, you may be thinking of the *Cheers* theme tune. You want parents, grandparents, and students alike to feel welcome; you want them to feel like they belong. You don't want them to think, "Oh no, it's karate later, I hate going to that place" (because it's cold, dirty, scruffy, or awkward). You want them to feel that you are there to help them. If you crack that piece of the puzzle, it will boost your retention of students, which contributes to your net monthly enrolment.

What is Guestology?

It's a term coined by Disney and refers to how they treat their 'guests' (any customer of Disney). I have read two books on Disney, and they are well worth the time invested. I am not going to explain in detail here fully, but you need to understand that EVERY single part of your students' experience needs to be engineered. You need to engineer each process so that it makes it as positive as possible for the students and their support network. When my team members started to understand this, they would tell me at the Monday all-team meeting if they had had a good or bad guestology experience that week outside of work. The worst ones were always car mechanics, who were probably great at fixing cars but terrible at putting themselves in their customers' shoes, and doctors' receptionists were a close second.

A few examples at your school would be:

- Guestology for their initial call.

- Guestology for getting the initial personal development pack to them.

- Guestology for their first-ever visit.

- Guestology for their second-ever visit, including their class experience.

- Guestology for their progress folder conference.

- Guestology for progress checks.

- Guestology for when they enter and leave your school (regardless of grade).

- When they need to use your bathrooms, make sure they are clean and stocked up.

There are MANY more frequently occurring situations that you need to have addressed and systemised. At some points during this book, you may be thinking, *"He's taking this a bit OTT, isn't he?"* That's the point though. If you want your school to stumble along and continue making zero or hardly any money, then keep doing what you have been doing. If you want to turn your part-time hobby into a full-time profession, then follow my advice. I've made zero money per month and made £35k+ per month; I know which one I would rather be at. As soon as you look after your students and go the extra mile, you will notice that your business becomes more successful. Trust me, I've done it. There's a saying I read once: *"Go the extra mile because there's no traffic there."*

How do you make them feel welcome?

- You need to know EVERY student's name. To do this, ensure that during your weekly meetings, a photo of any new enrolments is printed off and ready for your team (these then go on the 'Welcome to Our Newest Members' board). If you are the only instructor, then it's easy – it's all down to you. The pictures were brought to meetings for 8 weeks to ensure all team members knew faces. On the day a new student enrols, you also have a quick 'end of night' meeting where you confirm names of students who have enrolled.

- Pre-enrolment: When students are attending their first-ever lesson (i.e., their consultation), team members need to know the child's name and age (this is gathered on the initial enquiry sheet). It's also advisable to know the parent/guardian's name. Do not call them by their first name unless they insist. I always referred to people as Mr or Mrs unless they told me otherwise. Remember, this is a professional environment, and you need to establish that at the start. If you took your child to their parents' evening, the teacher should not really refer to you by your first name. There needs to be professionalism throughout your school.

- During their consultation: Kneel down and speak to the parents. Ask them how they found you, if their child is excited or nervous, put them at ease, and say you will look after them. Never tower over them. Remember the saying: *"Eye level is buy level."*

- During their first 3-8 lessons (i.e., 1-4 weeks), a member of the team should be assigned to welcome them into your school. You constantly want the parent support network to be amazed at how much you care. We called this the 'handholding' phase. This was not meant to be a derogatory term, but it was meant to remind team members that we need to look after them. We are martial artists who have been involved in the arts for a number of years, but to beginners, it's all alien: the mats, barefoot, loud noises, suits, bowing, etc.

- Get to know the parents. My team was encouraged to leave the mats for a few minutes if the other instructor could manage, to go and have 3-minute meetings with parents. These are just another positive touchpoint. I can explain how to carry out a sincere but quick 3-minute meeting, but now is not the time. The team member must not sit down because it's harder to keep within the 3-minute limit; they should kneel so they avoid getting too comfy.

Progress checks

These can be 10-25 minutes long. They are a check on the student's physical knowledge of your curriculum, but also their character development and self-discipline knowledge. This is your prime chance to give them high-fives, make them laugh, and praise them. I'm not saying be a jester, but it's your time to build on that relationship. Ask them how school is going, if they've done anything exciting recently, etc.

Progress checks are a great way to learn more about your student and build on your rapport. You may find out that they also attend scouts/beavers, and you have a marketing opportunity to follow up on. During our progress checks, we used to award our students a green tab, which had two purposes.

The first was so the students felt that they had achieved something. The second was for the other instructors to realise who had and had not had a progress check. They could then spend time with those who hadn't completed one. The progress checks could and should be done in mini-groups of 3-5 students. Following the progress check, the instructor can then briefly feedback to the parent what was good and what they recommend they work on.

This piece of the puzzle is important because it separates you from your standard 'sports coaches.' To be successful, though, you need to have a sincere feeling for your students' journey and their progression.

Progress Folder Conference

This is for students who have just enrolled in your school. Ideally, this takes place on their third visit: the first visit is their introductory consultation, the second is their second lesson and enrolment conference, and the third is when they have enrolled and are officially students. Both parents/guardians (or anybody involved in decision making) need to be present for this. It's your opportunity to demonstrate that you take their child's development seriously and want to provide them with the tools to benefit as much as possible.

During the progress folder conference, you explain in more detail your self-discipline sheets, your personal development books, your expectations for parents (e.g. they cannot 'dump and run' — meaning that parents should not drop their child off in the car park and then go shopping), your expectations for students, their first belt test, and much more.

The progress folder conferences #1 and #2 were a significant part of our team training because they are integral to your school's growth. The more you distance yourself from a seasonal recreation club, the more you cement your value in your parents' minds. You never want them to bracket us in with football, netball, rugby, cricket, dance, bouldering, etc. We are an integral part of a child's development. When we did lose a member, I would dig out their original new member photo, bring it to the all-team meeting, and let everyone know that we had failed that student.

We had not proved how valuable our programme was to their parent or guardian. Of course, sometimes situations were beyond our control — for example, they were moving away — but most times, we had dropped the ball. As a business owner, we need to take responsibility.

The 'How Was Karate?' Test

This is a question that many parents will ask their child in the car on the way home. You need to ensure the response from your child is: 'EXCELLENT – can't believe we have to wait three days to go back.' If the answer is 'erm… okay,' then you need to make your student feel more special. I'm not saying you should give them a certificate every single lesson or praise them when they don't deserve it. What I am saying is that your students need to have fun and learn your art at the same time. If they have done well during the lesson, finish off with a 'skills drill' — another piece of terminology. Do not refer to it as a 'game.' Your 'skills drill' is fun but also aims to improve some element of their physical training.

Stage Management

Going back to unwelcoming environments, when I was a young man, about 22, I was doing a lot of training in both karate and weight training. I used to travel with my weight training friends to local gyms we had heard of that sounded good. I remember one, where, when we walked in, it felt like someone had cut the loud music and told everyone to drop their weights and look at us two puny individuals at the start of our 'white belt' weightlifting journey. Imagine every one of your high-grade, brown and black belts, including your instructors, stopping immediately what they are doing and looking over at any newcomer who walks through the doors. It's not really the atmosphere you want.

If you run a school, regardless of whether it's tai chi or MMA, you need to work on your friendly and welcoming environment. Don't underestimate the importance of stage management. You only get one chance to make a first impression, so make sure it's as professional as possible. Remember that getting people through your front door is the hardest part, so for you to be successful, it needs to be properly stage-managed.

Negative Touch Points

- "What's your name again?"

- "Why can't you get this? It's the easiest technique we do. Everybody else has got it."

Or any other remark where you insinuate that the student is sub-standard. Money-specific ones are always bad:

- "Please can I have £20 for their next grading?"

- "Please can I have £30 for their annual membership?"

- "Please can I have £30 for their licence/insurance?"

- "Please can I have £10 for their pre-grading class?"

Every transaction or contact with you and your school is either putting money into their emotional bank account or taking it out. When you carry out team training, it's important to go over sayings that an instructor should never use. We would often practice the alternatives, which are less abrupt, at least five times as much. You don't want to practice your undesired behaviours — that's like practising how to do a kick wrong. You want to practice the desired behaviours in everything you do.

Have a Clean and Tidy School

This is a big part of guestology. You cannot charge a premium price point for your programme and expect parents not to notice the cleanliness of your school. Think about places you've been to where the cleanliness wasn't up to scratch — e.g. overflowing bins, wrappers on the floor, dust on picture frames/signs, fingerprints on mirrors and glass, or, the worst one, no toilet roll left. Your school needs to be clean and tidy all the time. Another one of our team sayings was: 'If we can see it, they can see it.' We trained CIT members to regularly walk the school and correct anything that was not as it should be. They had a CIT checklist that needed completing before and after every lesson.

I remember when I was a 1st Degree back in 1999, one of my Senseis frequently used to forget brown belt student names. This wasn't because he had a huge following, but because he hadn't really taken the time to reinforce the students' names in his mind. Imagine a parent had been coming to your school for three to four years, paying you every month for the past 36 to 48 months, and heard the instructor say: "What are you called again?" As a parent,

I would not be thrilled. I have been paying tuition every month for three to four years, and the instructor doesn't even know my son/daughter's name.

As a parent myself, I occasionally (0.001%) call my children by their sibling's name, but that's an honest mistake — that should be the only time you make that mistake with your students. This could be acceptable if you are the head/master instructor with an active count of over 400 students, don't teach regularly, and only see students once every three to six to twelve months.

In summary, to improve your school, you need to look at how your parents see it. Start to look at it from a parent's perspective and see where you can improve. Guestology is something that will separate you from others and allow your school to succeed.

Chapter 24

The Consultation Aka 'The Intro'

This is often the first physical/tangible experience of your school. If you have done things properly from the enquiry stage, you will have, at the bare minimum:

- Sent them an initial Personal Development pack

- Sent them an email with a link to a video of your school (with you explaining how your school will help their family)

- Telephoned them the day before and the day of

You should have already started to build rapport and begun to separate yourself from other seasonal recreation clubs. At every point during that initial sales process, you want them to think, 'Wow – I didn't expect this... these guys must be good,' etc.

The consultation should be a well-oiled process. Toilets should be freshly cleaned, the area sprayed with air freshener, chairs set out ready for your parents, 2nd Personal Development packs, and probably most importantly, a team member ready to welcome them into your school. Always be prepared for them; this is a valuable and crucial part of your school's overall success.

The consultation is the most important time of your day. This is the money hour; it should be referred to internally as the 'new business hour'. This is your chance to show your prospective students just how unique your school is and create overwhelming value. You only get one chance to make a first impression, so don't blow that first chance. Amaze them with your school, professionalism, and your unique programme.

Remember that your number one job is to market your school. When you get prospects into your school, you have done a great job. Well done, because that's the hardest part to master. Ensure that you and ALL your team realise how crucial this part of your school's growth is. At no point should a team member be looking at their phone or going to the toilet, leaving the front desk/front door unattended. We had a 'heads-up' policy, which meant that the person on the front desk must always be looking up and towards the entrance area.

The number one goal is for the child to have fun, closely followed by you providing an insane amount of value to the parent support network (i.e. the people who brought them).

What Not to Do (& What to Do)

- DON'T – Have a class running at the same time where they are doing sparring or anything that looks super aggressive, e.g. knife attacks.

  - You might love sparring and it might be a big part of your curriculum, but for some parents, it can shout out, 'They're going to teach my child to fight.'

- DON'T – Be too busy to speak to them because you are teaching.

  - Having a busy school is good, but somebody competent needs to be on hand to meet and greet them. You can build this into your schedule.

- DON'T – Cover absolutely every part of your syllabus during their consultation.

  - After we decided to stop throwing beginners into a normal class and expecting them to keep up, we created the intro. This was a good step, but I wanted to show them everything during that lesson. We taught them a few basics, kicking combinations, stance work, self-defence, pad work, board breaking – it was too much for them. With it being so physical, I was just putting us in the 'sports activity' category. They were having fun, but there was no real educational/developmental piece – it was just physical.

- DON'T – Start the lesson late.

   o If they have shown you respect by arriving at the time you told them to, then the least you can do is start the lesson on time. I like punctuality, so assume they do too.

- DON'T – Let them join in without completing the health & safety form.

   o Our H&S form had, on the reverse side, a Goals form. Before the consultation started, we would insist that it was completed. If we had time, we would then speak to them about how we could help them achieve their goals (if we could).

- DON'T – Let parents sit as far away from the intro as possible.

   o We had an intro room for 1:1 intros/consultations, but we also had group intros where we separated the mats off using free-standing bags and cones. In effect, we created two areas out of our one large area. Parents of intro students were expected to join in or sit down at a 90° angle to their child. If you sit them down behind their child, they do not get to see their child's face, which is hopefully beaming a large smile.

- DON'T – Just teach them kicks and punches and physical things from your art.

    o You need to teach them important aspects of your Personal Development journey. We taught them our Student Creed #1 whilst also engaging with parents on how this was important to their child. We also briefly covered our Success Quote and LIFE SKILL of the term. Peppered within that was reverse punch, rising block, front kick – that's it!

- DON'T – Be too strict and treat them like Black Belts.

    o Of course, you need to introduce respect and the bowing principle, which your parents should be impressed by, but at the same time, don't shout at them for fidgeting as you would do if they were Black Belts. Definitely raise the issue, but don't severely punish them. The students need to have fun, and at the same time, you introduce them to respect and discipline.

You need to look at your consultation process from a brand-new parent's perspective: why should they choose you over football, dancing, scouts, iPad, etc.? You want them to leave thinking, 'Wow – that place is amazing – I can't believe they will teach them all that whilst learning self-defence and getting physically fit.'

This is another chapter that I could have really expanded on because there are subtle things that you should do to ensure the value of your programme is clear to see during the consultation.

In summary, you must not throw your students into a normal class. They must attend a stage-managed and well-designed (& rehearsed) intro/consultation lesson. Team members delivering the intro need to be trained on exactly what to cover to create that value. Their number 1 job is to get a 100% success rate from 1st:2nd.

Chapter 25

Your Timetable & Lesson Types

This is another area of running my school that I messed up over and over again for the first 10 years. I want you to understand that, for me to grow my school to over £25k in tuition each month, I had to make and learn from many mistakes.

When designing your schedule, you need to design it with your ideal client in mind. For running a martial arts school, which is, for all intents and purposes, a grassroots-level organisation (meaning students come in as complete novices, having never worn a gi before), your ideal client (your avatar) is likely to be a 5–10-year-old child. They will probably enrol with a sibling, and 1 or 2 parents will tag along (since their tuition is 100% free anyway). Do not design it as if you are going to be overrun with Black Belts from day 1 (or even day 300). If you are just building your school, Black Belts won't be with you until after 3.5 years, maybe longer depending on your style.

All your lessons should be family classes. Now, before you say anything like, "Well, I'm a grappler, I can't have adults rolling with young kids," I understand that. But that is why you need to get the children involved and then enrol the adults too. I don't want to go too deep into class management, but you could have all ages in one group and then separate them down into mini-groups during that lesson. Do not mistake that for needing 3-4 instructors per group just because you are separating your class down into 4 groups. With an active count of probably 140, I taught every lesson and did not utilise any of my Black Belts nearly as much as I should have done. I was a super control freak, which limited my school's growth.

When I was doing things wrong, I used to run classes based on age: 3-5 years (Little Ninjas), 6-12 years (Junior Dragons), 13-16 years (Teens), and then adults. All you end up doing there is making it harder for parents with two children and not making it appealing for adults to enrol, as they only see one adult in the adult class. For any parents reading this, imagine if you had to take your child to a class at 6pm and then their sibling to another class at 7pm. Then, if you wanted to enrol, you have to come at a later time or a different day. You have 2 options:

a) Stay there for the 2 lessons back-to-back, which, as we know, is a juggling act to keep the other child busy while the other one is in class; or

b) Bring one child to class on a Monday, then the other on a Tuesday. Then, because they need to be there twice a week, you have to take them on Wednesday and Thursday.

So, what turned out to be a nice idea becomes an absolute chore. Parents have to be at your school 4 days a week. After finishing work, they must attend your school as a spectator most evenings. Now, I had many members who would love to be at my school 7 days a week, but let's not forget these are the small percentage. They are the hardcore students who love your art and, more than likely, you as an instructor.

So, as a business owner, you must look at it from your parents' point of view. Ask yourself this question: Am I making it easier or harder for my parents? Look at that small business "Amazon." A part of their huge success is the ease of being able to purchase items. They make the sales process as easy as possible for buyers. The parents are the decision-makers, or, more importantly, the bill payers. If the 6-year-old, the 10-year-old, and mum or dad can all train in the same class twice a week, then excellent. As a business owner, you need to be thinking about your retention. The more negative touchpoints there are, the more likely you are to lose students. You might not even enrol them because your timetable does not work for your ideal student families.

From running a school for over 20 years that grew each year, was profitable each year, and for 10 of those being very profitable, I have streamlined the process so you can avoid the negative touchpoints. Learn from my mistakes and adopt the success principles I have learned along the way.

Schedule Example:

An ideal schedule would be family classes at convenient times for your parents. You would then separate those down into levels, i.e., your grades/belts.

Please turn over the page for a schedule example:

Monday:

5pm = Family class, trial enrolment

6pm = Family class, Black Belt training

Tuesday:

5pm = Family class, Black Belt training

6pm = Family class, trial enrolment

(You would then repeat this format for Wednesday and Thursday)

Wednesday:

5pm = Family class, trial enrolment

6pm = Family class, Black Belt training

Thursday:

5pm = Family class, Black Belt training

6pm = Family class, trial enrolment

Friday:

Private lessons / progress checks / team training, etc.

Saturday:

10am = Family class, Black Belt training

11am = Family class, trial enrolment

We tried running classes earlier than 5pm, but they were never really well attended. The 5pm ones used to be big because parents would pick children up from school and get them to us quickly. We used to have 4 and 4.30pm slots just for progress checks and private lessons.

Never have all trial enrolment lessons or Black Belt training lessons at the same time. I used to have all my "Junior Dragon" classes at 5pm, Monday to Friday (another one of my many mistakes). The number of members I did not sign up (bad terminology used there) because "all my Junior Dragon classes were too early or too late" was astounding. Yet again, I left money on the table and probably let so many students not reap the benefits of regular martial arts tuition. They fell at the first hurdle, and it was 100% my fault.

You need to see-saw your timetable to reduce the number of rejections you will receive at the enrolment conference (better use of terminology there). So, if you say to parents, "We have an early or a later trial enrolment lesson," they will choose the one that fits in best with their schedule.

DO NOT create a schedule built to handle an active count of 350 if you only have 50 students. Add to your schedule as your net enrolment grows. There is nothing worse than an empty school. If I only had 50 students, I would hold lessons 2–3 days a week and only have 2 lessons a day at most. All your other time should be spent getting out and promoting your school (if you want it to be a success). So, on the evenings you aren't teaching, you should be delivering taster lessons at Scouts, Beavers, church groups, etc. Your lessons might be on Monday and Wednesday, which means you can organise to take part in marketing on Tuesday, Thursday, and Friday evenings.

Your schedule grows and evolves as your school's active count grows. At our peak, we had 22 timetabled lessons a week. Now, remember though, it's quality, not quantity. We could have had 30–40 lessons a week and only had a handful of students in each. We instead wanted our school to be energetic and for fellow students to feel that they were part of something. A nice class size for us was 20–25 students.

What is Trial Enrolment and Black Belt Training?

I expand on these later in the book, but here is a very brief overview.

Trial Enrolment: This is the programme that all your brand-new students attend when they enrol in your school (there is more on this programme later in the book). You want them to enjoy the training and not regret enrolling in your school. They need to look forward to every lesson and leave after every lesson with a big smile on their face. The last thing you want is for them to enrol and, on their next lesson—their first proper lesson as an official student—have a bad experience. During the first 2–3 months, you need to hold their hand and acclimatise them to your school. I covered this more in the guestology section. You want them to enjoy the lessons and start learning the basics. Your role is not to make them the best yellow or orange belt ever. Your number-one aim in this programme is to get them to see how valuable it is to train for Black Belt and, subsequently, to commit to becoming a Black Belt.

Black Belt Training Programmes: There are two different lessons/programmes for all students who have made that commitment to become a Black Belt. If you committed to training for Black Belt, you either enrolled in our highest-level programme, named 'Masters & Leadership', or 'Black Belt Training'. Again, there are many subtle differences between the Black Belt training programmes and the basic training (a.k.a. trial enrolment programme). The lessons are often 15 minutes longer, there is a more advanced curriculum, the personal development content is deeper, but the main difference is that the students wear a different uniform. Students cannot just enrol in this programme at the enrolment conference—they need to genuinely qualify to be accepted into the programme. I will discuss this in more detail in the 'Trial Enrolment and Black Belt Training Programme' section later in this book. There are quite a few moving pieces to ensure this part of your school runs.

A & B Days

You may have read about A and B days and want to keep that or bring it in. That's fine, but do not let the students know when the A and B days are. If you do, you will have everybody who loves sparring turning up on those days early, and those who hate sparring turning up on the non-sparring days. This will then have a knock-on effect at your gradings, where their standard is weighted more towards their particular strength. We all know that, as martial arts instructors, your foundations are absolutely crucial to your success. In karate, it is having a good, strong, solid stance; for your particular style, it is likely something else. However, that element cannot be taught just on a particular day.

A quick note on class management and running order: You or your team need to follow a simple system for the type of warm-up to cover each lesson and what content to cover. You can't have instructors varying too much in what they teach. You don't want one instructor doing a boring 25-minute warm-up and then another doing a super-high-intensity 5-minute warm-up, etc. Before I carried out team training, this is exactly what happened. There was no consistency between the two instructors I used to let teach. I designed a class management system that provided instructors with the warm-up and content for each lesson. It was, of course, a rotation so that not every class was the same. Doing this, though, made sure there were no large gaps in standard come testing time because one instructor had taught their favourite area for the previous grading cycle.

In summary, hopefully, this chapter has made it a bit clearer on how your timetable should look on a weekly basis. You should not have separate junior, teens, and adult classes, but you should offer family classes. Your family classes are then separated down into trial enrolment or Black Belt training programmes. The only students that can attend your Black Belt training programme lessons are those who have made the commitment to become a Black Belt at your school.

Chapter 26

'Trial Enrolment' and Your 'Black Belt Training' Programmes

For the first 14 years of running my school, I did things the old-fashioned way—the way that my instructor did it, and the way his instructor did it before him. This may be how you're running your school right now. I can imagine the format has not changed since the early 1960s, when Karate was introduced to the UK. You might be following the same system and thinking, as I once did, "Well, if it was good enough for me when I was a student, then surely it's good enough for my students." Wrong!

Was your instructor running a highly successful school? Was it a systemised business that operated without their day-to-day input? Or were they really just self-employed? Imagine how many hundreds, probably thousands, of students started but never achieved the coveted Black Belt. Yes, I 100% agree that achieving Black Belt should be hard, a challenge, and should weed out those who don't work hard. However, it is our job as instructors to develop those transferable LIFE SKILLS—skills such as perseverance, determination, discipline, grit, resilience, and more.

At no point should your students be able to drop into any class they want, and for us as instructors to just hope and pray they stay around until Black Belt. That mindset kills your school's growth. This was another mistake I made; I just hoped and wished that students would stay around.

Your schedule should not be like mine was in my early days. Something like this:

Monday

Mixed grades: 6–7 pm

Mixed grades: 7–8 pm

Wednesday

Mixed grades: 6–7 pm

Mixed grades: 7–8 pm

Saturday

Mixed grades: 9–10 am

Mixed grades: 10–11 am

Yes—every class was open to any grade and any age. I thought I was giving my students and parents flexibility, which is good, isn't it? Giving students and parents options is good, but only when they align with your school's mission.

Why should it not be like this?

You're giving your students too much choice. Think of swimming lessons: when your child progresses, they have to attend a different lesson. Think of the school structure: after Year 1, you move to Year 2; then, after Year 2, you move to Year 3, and so on. The actual days and times of your school don't change, but your curriculum does.

In some of your classes, you may have a 5-year-old white belt with a short attention span who needs a lot of direction and support (nothing wrong with that), and you may have some brown and Black Belts who need your time for their upcoming grading. Like you, I thought of myself as a very good instructor. I could handle big classes of mixed grades and abilities because I was good at my craft; I'd earned trophies, awards, and recognition for my coaching.

The first change you need to make in your schedule is separating it down into 'trial enrolment' lessons and 'Black Belt training' lessons.

When students first enrol in your school, they enrol in the trial enrolment programme. They cannot enrol in any higher-level programme. The only students who can attend the trial enrolment lessons are those who have not yet committed to becoming a Black Belt or those who have committed but are still within their first 12 months with you. Students who have committed should be wearing the relevant coloured jacket. This means the highest grade you can ever have in that programme is the highest belt a student can achieve with you after one year of training. For my school, that was white belt - purple stripe.

Remember, though, that trial enrolment is only a one-year programme. They cannot continue after one year; they have either decided and committed to becoming a Black Belt or not. This took me ages to understand—I was programmed the old way. We can't just tell students they can't continue; parents will be upset, and everybody will leave (wrong mindset again). This is all down to the education and pre-framing of your parents during the enrolment process. Parents are told several times that they are on a trial enrolment programme, and it's their opportunity to decide if they want to train for Black Belt and beyond, PLUS for us to decide if we would like to work with them for 4–5 years. We have a separate belt display showing all the trial enrolment belts and the order they go in; it clearly shows the highest belt they could achieve.

I don't want you to think too deeply about the programme differences yet, but the main differences between your programmes should be similar to this.

Trial enrolment programme	**Committed to Black Belt programmes**	
	Black Belt Training	**Masters and leadership**
Max belt; white belt-purple stripe	Up to 1st Black Belt	Up to 2nd Black Belt
45 minutes	60 minutes	60 minutes
Max 12 months	3-year programme	5-year programme
Wear a black suit	Wear the same jacket at the sensei	
Very basic curriculum	More advanced curriculum inc kata + sparring+ Weapons	
2 personal development books	Lots of pd books CIT eligibility	

There are so many differences between the trial enrolment programme and the Black Belt programmes. I was so stubborn and didn't act for ages. Rather than adopt what highly successful schools were doing, I second-guessed everything. I had the wrong mindset, which hindered our school's growth, professionalism, and profits. For years, I squashed my school's success. If I had acted sooner, our school's active count would have grown, our dropout rate would have reduced, and we would have had a better bottom-line figure. If you are not renewing students to a higher-level programme (where the benefits far outweigh the additional cost), then you are doing them a disservice and leaving money on the table. Please don't stand in your own way like I did – just act.

Your next steps after reading this book should be to increase your marketing, create a marketing plan, amend your schedule, and seek professional mentorship (check out my website if you want to learn more). I have a clearly laid-out roadmap for you to take your school to the next level and beyond. I want my mentees to achieve a huge spike in net enrolments within 4-6 weeks of working with me. Typically they grow by 10-50 members depending on what they implement.

Staging of your school

It should be clear to parents who enter your school that there is a clear difference between the programmes. They might not be able to explain the difference, but you want parents to say things like:

- 'How does my child earn their red jacket?'

- 'When can my child apply for Black Belt training?'

- 'Do they only do weapons on the Black Belt programmes?'

- 'Do they cover other personal development books in the other programme?'

My school had 3-4 belt displays. One of the belt displays showed all the belts a student could earn in the trial enrolment programme. These were all striped belts, and we had 6 (based on the students grading every 2 months). They were:

- White-red stripe

- White-yellow stripe

- White-orange stripe

- White-green stripe

- White-blue stripe

- White-purple stripe

This is a super clear distinction. Students on the Black Belt training programmes wore full-colour belts. We still had striped belts, but there were white stripes running through the full-colour belts and they were earned halfway through, i.e. 2 months into a grading cycle.

The suits between trial enrolment and the Black Belt training programmes are different. Trial enrolment students wore black suits, but those committed to earning their Black Belt wore the same colour jacket as our Senseis – this was red. Don't get too bogged down in the colours; it's more about you understanding there needs to be a difference.

In about 2007, one of the ground-breaking changes I brought in was that all beginners wore black suits, but then when you achieved blue belt, you wore a white suit. This wasn't particularly ground-breaking, since it was my club and I could introduce whatever suits I wanted, but this was partly because I had read in a magazine that it was just another way to earn some money from existing members. Again, the complete wrong way to look at it.

After being mentored by true professionals in the industry, I found out this was small-time thinking. Yes, it introduced a few more pounds, but it hardly catapulted the school's gross income and profitability. Please don't step over pounds to pick up pennies. This applies to your personal growth too – invest in knowledge.

For those of you who don't know too much about me, I have a property portfolio which ticked along at a snail's pace for about 15 years. As soon as I committed to learning more about property, my portfolio doubled in the first year and then doubled again the year after. Yes, I had to pay for mentorships and 3-4 day intense courses, but without a doubt, that knowledge opened the door to growing my property portfolio, cash flow, and wealth. I have spent well over £100,000 on just my Martial Arts mentorship. However, I made more than triple that back – again, it links back to ROI.

I could go on in more depth here about how the curriculum advances, how the personal development books expand, and how the lesson format is slightly different, but this chapter is about you understanding that you HAVE to have 2 separate programmes: a trial enrolment programme and a Black Belt training programme, if you want to plug your dropout rate and get more students to Black Belt. As soon as you start to educate your parents on just how beneficial a Black Belt journey at your school is to their child, you will have more and more students committing to your Black Belt programmes.

Part 5
OPERATIONS

Chapter 27

What a Typical Day Should Look Like If You Want To Grow Your School

You don't stumble across success

If you are serious about growing your school, which I'm sure you are, otherwise you wouldn't be reading this book, then you need to plan your days, weeks, months, and years. You don't just stumble across success; you won't wake up one day with an active count of 300 and a high monthly tuition. You must plan for success and work towards it every day. The fact that you are willing to learn how to improve your school is a huge step. Compare your mindset and attitude to the thousands of school owners who say they want more students but don't bother learning how to build a profitable school – you're a step ahead.

Before you start planning your year and months, you need to work backwards; i.e., you need to plan your day. Your typical day should consist of these high-value tasks:

- Marketing (gathering leads/enquiries)

- Confirmation calls (getting prospects into your school)

- 1st lesson delivery (showing them the true value of your unique programme)

- 2nd lesson delivery and enrolment conferences

- Retention of students (teaching and retaining students)

- Tracking stats (knowing how your business is doing)

Notice that the above are high-value tasks. There is no mention of cleaning and organising the office. Of course, cleaning is important, and nobody should have a scruffy, dirty school, but cleaning should be done at the end of the day with the help of your CITs. Organising the office/front desk should not take much time if everybody is following the systems you have in place and putting things back where they should go after using them.

Marketing

The more you focus on marketing, the more leads you will get. Now, this is not a linear relationship. You will find that some marketing efforts far outperform others. For instance, when we attended garden centres on a Saturday, we had a steady trickle of leads, but when we went to a cinema for a big film release, there were times we couldn't keep up with the flow. Likewise, we attended some events that were excellent lead generators, but when we attended the following year, they fell flat. Your marketing is expanded on more in the marketing section, but every day you should be doing something to generate new business for your school.

Again, do not overthink this at first. Don't be thinking, "I need to rebuild my website, employ a marketing and PR agency, up my SEO game, design fancy business cards," etc. You must understand, however, that this high-value task should not be pushed aside for a lower-value task. Don't neglect goal-achieving activities by completing tension-relieving tasks. Many people get to the end of the day or week and feel like they have been busy, but when you look at it in detail, they have not been productive or effective. Always ask yourself: is this a goal-achieving action or just keeping me busy, i.e., tension-relieving? You can judge your success not by how many hours you've worked, but by how effective you've been at generating leads for your school. Leads are the lifeblood of your school – if you don't have them coming in, your school is slowly dying.

You want to, at a bare minimum, have a few leads coming in every week, and as you improve, a few leads coming in every day. It is possible; you just need to be willing to work. Another mistake I made at certain points was slacking off the marketing and only relying on 2-3 sources. I thought we were comfortable and at a steady gross, so we put the marketing off for a month or two. We still had the SEO running, but this was still a big mistake. If you ever think your classes are getting too full, do not stop or reduce your marketing. If anything, I would say to spend more on it and take it to the next level.

If you are gaining new students at a rate you have never seen before, then do not go out and upgrade your car or lifestyle. Instead, pour all the extra money into marketing. The ideal position you want to be in is, "I don't know what to do with all these white belts."

Confirmation Calls (getting them into your school)

This was done as soon as a team member started their shift. We had 'first-hour jobs,' which were known as FHJs among the team. The instructor would come in, make confirmation calls for that day and anyone scheduled for the day after. They would also return any missed calls and text messages. This was only scheduled for an hour, so as soon as the FHJs had been done, they moved on to some sort of marketing task. The FHJs often took less than one hour, but the team knew that they only had a maximum of one hour to complete those tasks. Again, run your school efficiently.

The marketing tasks that week were based on our marketing calendar and were covered during the Monday team meeting/training. Do not underestimate the need to over-communicate with your team. You need to ensure everybody knows what they are doing and when they are doing it. As our team grew, I realised that I had to communicate more and more. If you are a one-person show, then excellent – it's down to you. As your team expands, make it crystal clear what you expect from them and what their performance is based on. For us, and for your school, that should be net enrolment, renewal rate, retention, and monthly gross. Yes, there are more measures, but those are the key ones.

1st Lesson Delivery (showing them the true value of your programme)

When we were open seven days a week, we had consultation slots every day. We wanted to overcome any objection from parents that delayed them from visiting our school. Objections included anything from, "Well, they have swimming then," "They're at their dad's on that night," or "They do football then." If, upon giving the prospect 3-4 slots, we would be honest with them and say that we have the biggest schedule in the area, so maybe just this once, miss one of their prior commitments and we guarantee they won't be disappointed. This, again, is down to your passion, enthusiasm, and belief in your programme and your school.

The best examples were when we would receive a call early on Monday, they would then attend the day after (Tuesday), and then have enrolled by Wednesday. We often booked students in for the same day if we felt we had enough time to hand-deliver their personal development pack. Hand-delivering packs takes your service to another level. Do you think any "seasonal recreation" sports clubs hand-deliver packs?

You should not have just one single slot for consultations, i.e., just Saturdays. You are alienating a large percentage and restricting your growth when a parent says, "I can't do Saturdays because we have football, my daughter goes swimming, my husband works, we go to our caravan." If you are holding lessons on two days a week so far, then you should have consultations on those days. You're there anyway, so hold them before and after your normal lessons. Do not just invite them to take part in your normal lesson and let one of your Black Belts (or higher grades) spend time with them. I, of course, made this mistake years ago. Again, I didn't appreciate how crucial that "new business" was.

Your assistant may be the nicest person in the world and/or they may be the most technically gifted, but they are not you. The best person to sell the benefits of your programme is you. If you have first-time students join a regular class, they are not being educated on everything you want to tell them. You cannot talk to their parents throughout, and you cannot speed up or slow down the lesson depending on their ability.

Your consultation is your opportunity to explain the benefits of your programme. During the consultation, ask questions like, "Mum/Dad – do they normally focus like this?" or "Mum/Dad – what we do here at our school is teach students about Respect, Discipline, and Determination. Do you think Bob would benefit from our programme?"

I could really expand on consultation delivery and how to create immense value, but this is not the time to do so. I just want you to design your school so that it gives you the best chance of enrolling lots of students.

2nd lesson delivery and enrolment conferences

Every day, you should be hosting second-lesson students. This will only happen if your marketing mix is firing on all cylinders and your consultation delivery is creating amazing value.

The second-lesson experience is another key process that you need to continually train on. You should be training team members on:

- Exactly what to say to the parents and the students

- Where to position themselves and at what time

- How, when, and where to award their white belt

The second lesson is your opportunity to build upon what the student learned in their first visit and to demonstrate to the parents (again) that you are professionals who teach transferable LIFE SKILLS. Having Black Belts there to help the student is excellent. You will be able to tell parents that you can help with respect, discipline, manners, leadership, and confidence. But when they see a Black Belt demonstrating those skills, it creates real value. When I personally delivered CIT training, I would say to the students, "You need to be a product of the product." If, after being with you for more than four years, they are showing everything you said you could teach, then you need to 'show off' your Black Belts to prospective parents.

The enrolment conference is simply a quick chat with the parents to briefly go over the programme while also getting them to confirm that:

a) They can see their child benefitting from your provision

b) They do want them to enrol

c) They can do two lessons per week

Throughout the enrolment conference, you should be getting little 'yes' responses from the parents—buying signals. The price presentation is then given, and you ask for the sale, i.e., saying something like, "Let's go and get Bob all set up on his new journey." Remember, though, that you are not strong-arming them during the enrolment conference. They should already be convinced of the value of your programme.

I could deliver a morning's worth of training on the EC, but I want you to understand that the EC is just the final step of the enrolment puzzle. If you and your team have done your job properly, the parents will be able to see the amazing value and want to enrol. The EC does need to have a contrast sale in place. For example, if you enrol after your second lesson, then we give you a £X discount. It should be £Y, but because you are enrolling now, it will be £Z, saving you £X.

Retention of Students (Teaching and Retaining Students)

There is no point in enrolling lots of members only to have them all leave within the first few weeks and months. When we really started to dig into our retention, we found out that 51% of our members did not make it to the end of Year 1. They were dropping out mainly at months 3-4, which is when the novelty wore off, and it was also when free sparring took place. You will find it very hard to build a successful school if your entire active count is turning over every two years. The 'churn' is too much.

I would just like to say here that this is before we had introduced any of our Black Belt programmes. It was a classic 'all grades, all ages' schedule design. Before the introduction of the Black Belt programmes, we were just doing a stupid model of '1 lesson a week is £x', '2 lessons a week is £y', and '3 lessons a week is £z'. What a stupid mistake. We were just cementing ourselves into every other sport activity. We were training parents to think of us as a 'cost per lesson' mentality.

When you enrol in university, your tuition is not calculated on the number of hours in class. The tuition and cost of the education are based on the desired outcome and the associated doors that degree will open. I have a degree and a PGCE, but I think that if I had my time again, I would just go straight into the real world at 16, educate myself through books and mentors that would help me in the field I wanted to excel in. I learned a lot at university and during my formal post-graduate studies, but I learned far more through self-education, mentorship, and being coached by top businesspeople. I can comfortably say that my self-education has benefited my family and me more than my formal education did. Remember Jim Rohns quote 'formal education will make you a living, self-education will make you a fortune'.

The biggest tool to help retain more students is to have them commit to becoming a Black Belt, i.e., they enrol in one of your Black Belt training programmes. I identify several retention tools in the retention section of this book, so I won't go over them here.

The most important way to keep hold of your students is to genuinely care for them. You need to understand that people buy from people, they don't buy from businesses. Show them that you care by spending a few minutes with them before or after a class. Chat to them about how they are getting on in life outside your school. As a martial arts instructor, your job is not just to teach them your art twice a week; your job is to try and mentor them to be the best version of themselves. This sincerity needs to be something your parents can see and something that any team members you have also possess. Think of any great coach or leader—they know how to get the best out of their team but also know more about their home life, etc.

Whenever I used to speak to the younger students (aged 3-12), I always used to teach them things I wanted my own children to know. For example, "Don't hang around with five idiots, or you will be the sixth."

Tracking Stats (Knowing How Your Business Is Doing)

This is done at the end of the day, and it tells you how well your school is doing. If you have had no leads or enquiries, then you need to do more marketing. If your first lessons didn't book for a second lesson, then that is a major concern that team training needs to take place immediately on your first lesson process and delivery. If your second lessons did not enrol because they were not prepared, then that is also first lesson training. If the EC failed, then that's down to second lesson delivery, the EC script, and/or educating your parents properly.

Without knowing your numbers, you are just sailing on open water without any control—you're just drifting around with no clear course. I can assure you that no successful business has just drifted around. Businesses that drift around are those that are often the walking dead. They have good months and bad months, but there is no increase in business month on month and year on year. You must track your stats and keep graphs, which are a visualisation of the figures. The trend should always point up. A plateau is just the same as a decline, it's just not as visible.

The more tools you bring into team meetings to show the team how good or bad they are doing, the better. Use colour markers on your flip chart paper: red means bad, and green means good.

Don't do admin-based tasks during the day. We used to do them at the end of the day so that they don't eat into the day's important tasks. Look into Parkinson's Law, and you will see why.

In summary, you need to only spend time on high-value activities during your day. If you are looking at massively increasing your membership, then you need to spend more time on marketing. The marketing you do will directly impact the success of your school. Whatever you do, do not sit in your school all day cleaning and complaining you have no students—get marketing.

Chapter 28

How Your School Should Look

I have mentioned many times throughout this book that you should be charging appropriately for the true value of your programme, and not bundling yourself in with other seasonal recreational pastime sports. Your true value is based on the benefits of your programme, or more accurately, the transformation that happens within each of your students the longer they stay with you.

Your school should look clean, tidy, and resemble a proper Black Belt School. This was not us from 2004-2007. I rented scout huts, a dance studio in a college, a rowing club/function room – you may be able to relate. I used to have to turn up an extra 30 minutes earlier than usual, just to check the area was clean. I remember numerous times arriving at about 8.30 am for a 10 am lesson, just to check that the bar staff had tidied the function room, including the entrance, hall, and toilets, the night before. If you don't have your own venue, you can still make changes to raise the professionalism of your school. At first, this took me a long time to understand.

If a parent walked into your school, would they know immediately that it is a Black Belt School? What does a Black Belt School even look like? Our school had the following:

- Banners

- Roll-up banners

- Posters on display

- Commitment sheets from your students

- Belt racks

- Our students' work

- Welcome board for all new members

- Committed board for all those committed to becoming a Black Belt

- Our credentials and achievements

Plus much more.

Does your venue just look like a typical scout hut – dusty, with a hard floor, no marketing material anywhere, and just your notepad and pen rested on a foldable table where you collect money each lesson? Don't worry, because this was me for the first few years. I then invested in one roll-up stand, which, looking back, had a terrible design. However, it raised the professionalism just a little bit. I then invested in a couple more a few months later. I used to place one in the entrance way, and another near where my desk was. At the end of my lessons, I would just pack them away and put them in the boot of my car. Eventually, I had five roll-up displays, small tabletop stands, and even A3 laminated posters that I used to take to each of my venues.

Level Up for Your Success

In 2010, when we moved into our own venue, I had to level up again. It was very sporadic and mismatched back then, but I was confident it still did the job of raising our professionalism. From 2019 onwards, my school was over-decorated, but I wanted it to be absolutely clear to even first-time visitors that we were a Black Belt School. I wanted them to walk in and think, 'Wow – this is better than Karate Bob's place near our house.'

Black Belt School Everywhere, All the Time

Being a Black Belt School was mentioned on the phone during the enquiry call and both confirmation calls. It was mentioned in the Initial Personal Development packs, in the video they were sent, during their 1st and 2nd meet-and-greet, during the EC, and many more times. But the most crucial part was during our intro/consultation lesson. That's when you should really have your students and parents' undivided attention. Parents needed to know that we expected students to stay and achieve Black Belt and beyond. We didn't scare them, but we planted important seeds for them to think about us as a serious educational component of their child's development, not just a 'we'll see how they get on' type of sport. We didn't want to be bundled into the "pay-as-you-play" category.

Parents are not looking for £1,000,000 worth of chrome fitness equipment and state-of-the-art changing rooms. Just think, what would this even do? It would put us in the gym bracket, and that is somewhere you definitely do not want to be. I have two of those budget gyms in my town that are open 24 hours a day. They both cost less than £20 per month for unlimited access, with state-of-the-art equipment and a huge free-weight area. You do not want to put yourself in that bracket. You need to firmly establish yourself in the 'education' part of your parents' minds. If you put yourself in the fitness part of their mind, you are massively underselling yourself and sabotaging your school's chance of success.

Your school should contain most of these:

- 2-3 banners: 'We are a Black Belt School'

- 2-3 banners: 'A Black Belt is a white belt that never quit'

- 2-3 banners: 'Goals + Commitment = Success'

- Students' work – their A1 or A2 Black Belt visualisation sheets

- Students' work – their A4 'I am going to be a Black Belt' posters

- Students' work – any achievement-type certificates they have earned at school, especially copies of school reports

- Black Belt wall with pictures of all students committed to Black Belt

Self-Discipline Items

- All the self-discipline sheets you use throughout your grading cycle: Reading, Homework, Healthy Eating, Self-Discipline, Job List

- Bonus self-discipline sheets you do during the year: Money Management, Emotional Regulation, Do It the First Time, Clean Your Room, Screen Time, plus much more

- Self-discipline medals and trophies need to be on display, maybe in two locations so parents have a greater chance of seeing them

- Pictures of successful students earning LOTS of medals and trophies, along with corresponding victory notes (taken from previous graduations)

Other items that are not Black Belt-specific but still help cement you as an educational activity, and therefore different, include:

- Banner: Conceive… Believe… Achieve

- A selection of your Personal Development books that students read. We used to have these near our 'Success Wall'

- Whiteboards with your Success Quote and LIFE SKILL of the Term

Yes, the above might seem like a lot if you are currently in a bland-looking scout hut, but trust me – just introduce 1-2 things a month. I have a clear strategy to help school owners improve their position, programme, and profits. The roll-up stands can be erected within 1 minute. You could get whiteboards, about A1 size, and just leave them in a safe space when your classes are not on. Take action now, don't procrastinate. Don't look at it as spending money – look at it as investing in your business, which in turn is an investment in your life.

It needs to be clear across your parents' first two visits that you are not just a 'here today-gone tomorrow' club. They need to see that you are committed to improving their child's future. Think of how a school classroom looks – you need similar vibes running through your school. When your existing parents see you starting to introduce these new ideas, it will feel different, but they should take it all on board. It should demonstrate that you are committed to improving your school. For any new parent who walks through the door, they will know no different; to them, this is how you have always done it.

If you have young children and you've ever looked into taking them to companies that help them with their academic work, that is how you want to position yourself. Yes, your child will have fun and learn your martial art, but combined with that, we will teach them Focus, Discipline, Respect, Perseverance, the ability to not give in to negative peer pressure, etc. You are not introducing desks and chairs, but there must be times in your lesson where you impart lessons on personal development, growth, success, etc.

I have hundreds of pictures of my school and how it evolved over the years. Ultimately, your school needs to look professional. You want parents to leave your school thinking, 'Wow, I didn't expect that... Everything was nice and friendly, and they seem really professional,' leaving no doubt that they will return and enrol.

Bigger is not necessarily better

Do not think that getting a bigger facility automatically means you will gain more members. When we moved into our school, I had a crazy idea of renting an 11,000 sq. foot unit. I was just caught up in the thought of "imagine how many students we could have in here," rather than "I've got to find this rent money every single month before I've enrolled anybody." Thankfully, we did not sign the lease. We moved into a unit that was approximately 2,750 square feet. If I were in that position again, I would not go above 2,000 square feet because I would want every inch of the area to be utilised. I know that I could comfortably run a 300-student active count school from 2,000 square feet (probably 1,500 square feet). I know what size matted area we should have, how big the front desk should be, where the lead instructor should stand, where stock should go, and the best places for parents to sit, etc.

At the end of the day, your school will be empty from 8 a.m. to 4 p.m., five days a week. Any extra space is just dead money, unless you have purchased your venue. This was going to be our next step, and my property company would have purchased the property, with my school paying the property company (me) the rent. Everything would have been legal and above board, but in doing so, the money would have stayed within my ecosystem. If you want any advice on property investing, that is another passion of mine. I can provide you with some tips on what to purchase to get the best returns.

In summary, the way your school is presented will have an impact on your growth. Just implement one thing at a time and you will notice the difference.

Chapter 29

How Your Students Should Look

As with any decent school, you want your students to be uniform. You want them all to wear the full uniform appropriate to their programme. For us, this meant that students on our trial enrolment programme wore our branded black suits with yellow print and embroidery. When they committed to Black Belt, they then wore one of two uniforms, depending on the programme they enrolled in. The Black Belt Training programme, which took students to 1st degree, saw them wear the traditional white gi with black print and embroidery. For the Master & Leadership students, who had committed to 2nd Degree Black Belt (our highest-level programme), they wore white pants and the exclusive red jacket, which was the same colour as our instructors' jackets.

Don't get bogged down in the colours they need to wear; it's the principle you need to understand. Each programme needs to have a different suit, and the highest-level programme needs to wear the same colour jacket as their Sensei. Remember, for many young students, their martial arts instructor will be like a superhero – so if they get to wear the same jacket as their instructor, it's an amazing experience for them.

Tied in with this is the expected behaviour of students when they wear the same jacket as their Sensei. When they renewed their membership, they didn't just receive the jacket; they had to earn it by completing various self-discipline tasks over the next 2-3 weeks. Doing so was another way to emphasise that we wanted learning to take place outside our four walls.

Behaviours you want them to learn:

- To carry their bag into your school and not burden their parents with it.

- To put their shoes/socks neatly on the racks provided.

- To stand still in class, bow on and off the area, and raise their hand if they have a question.

- To open doors for others.

- To help anyone who needs assistance, such as a grandmother or grandfather in the supermarket.

- For higher grades to welcome and get to know the younger grades.

Plus much more.

All the behaviours above were helping shape them into kind, caring, and thoughtful individuals.

If you have adopted the initial investment at the enrolment conference, your students will also be wearing their small kit bags and bringing in their water bottles (the progress folder we had printed was also a branded booklet). Everything feasible that you can brand, do so: suits, kit bags, water bottles, pens, pencils, hoodies, etc. When we really started to grow, we began ordering our equipment from Pakistan. This way, everything came to us branded, meaning we didn't have to order it from a UK supplier (with their logo on) and then send it off to be branded. I loved the look of our own belts, headguards, and mitts with our logo on. I felt it just elevated us that little bit more.

If it's every team member's role to market and promote the school, then surely you want your students—who should outnumber your team by 20:1, 50:1, maybe even 100:1—to also take part in that marketing. If your students are wearing your branded hoodies and suits, they will be seen by the neighbours at home, at the supermarket, when picking up their siblings from gymnastics, etc.

Your students should look neat and tidy, as it contributes to your 'esprit de corps'. Your students need to be little marketing ambassadors for your school.

Chapter 30

Your Enrolment Process

Put simply, this is what separates the professional schools from the amateur clubs.

You need to be able to identify exactly how a student enrols in your school. You need to be able to take this from the marketing stage to the enrolment. When you start to grow your team, they also need to know each stage of the enrolment process. For instance, this is a very basic enrolment process for our school:

1. We market (through various means) for new students.

2. A new student contacts us (via email, text, call, Facebook, or by dropping in).

3. We book them in for an intro (consultation).

4. They attend the intro and get booked in for a second lesson.

5. They attend the second lesson, have an enrolment conference, and enrol.

Now, the above is the absolute bare bones of the process. There are many more moving parts. It should give you an idea of what your enrolment process should look like. My enrolment process back in 2004 was to put 10 posters in shops and pray that students would come to my club. When they did turn up, I briefly spoke to the parents, handed them a health & safety form, didn't ask anything about what they were hoping to achieve for their child, and just threw them into class, hoping they would keep up. There was no clear structure on how they became a member. I often just let them pay £4 per lesson until they didn't come back or asked me how to join. I didn't know anything about the sales principle of 'ABC' back then. You need to be in control of the sales process. Students cannot just keep attending until they decide to enrol. There is a clear process they need to follow.

Let's not forget how alien a martial arts environment is to a non-martial artist. People don't wear shoes, there are people bowing all the time, they wear funny-looking uniforms and belts, there is no messing around or banter as might be the case in other team sports, you call the instructor Sensei/Sifu/Master, there are loud shouts, etc. I mention this because the parents may think what they are doing is correct, i.e. they haven't been asked to enrol yet, so they must not be ready.

Action = Results

I honestly don't know how I gained my first few members because of the lack of marketing knowledge I had, but I took action, and it got results. Albeit small results, but I got them. That is a very important theme when trying to develop and enhance your business: Don't spend months planning the curriculum, your logo, or your website. Just do things that get members! Action = Results!

This is how our enrolment process looked from 2018 onwards:

1. **We market for new students.**

   Through a variety of media: Facebook ads, SEO, lead generation events, signs near our school, a flag at the bottom of our street, direct mail, primary school leaflets, primary school enrichment programmes, Boy Scout tasters, Girl Guide tasters, bag packing in supermarkets, signs on railings, and much more (+ internal marketing such as parties, graduations, special seminars, buddy week, etc.).

2. **A new student contacts us.**

We then follow a clearly defined phone script (or email if their enquiry was via email or Facebook). We inquire about their goals for enrolment and confirm whether we are a good fit for each other. We then send them an information pack (yes, a physical pack—don't be penny-pinching), plus we send them a text with a link to our 'Congratulations, you've booked your first lesson' web page and an email containing the same information. Some elements of this are hand-written to help with the 'wow' factor.

3. **We book them in for an intro (consultation).**

We contact them 24 hours before their consultation and go over our clearly defined script to ensure we are preparing them for their consultation. We then contact them on the day to ensure both parents are still attending and to go over the script from the day before. Calling them on the day is even more important if we did not manage to speak to them the day before.

4. **They attend the intro (consultation) and get booked in for a second lesson.**

They are met in the car park or outside our front doors. We build rapport and walk them into our school. They take part in a LIFE SKILL and Character Development lesson, which clearly shows parents that we are not just another seasonal recreational club but a key part of a child's development. The lesson is fun because, ultimately, the children need to enjoy it. We then provide them with another pack of information explaining what will happen in their second lesson, plus we provide them with some self-discipline homework. The self-discipline homework is a game changer because, to my knowledge, no other 'seasonal recreational sport' does this. Once again, we are separating ourselves from the 'sport' mentality. We are having an impact on their child outside the four walls of our school. They get a confirmation call 24 hours before their second lesson, and team members follow a clearly defined script so we can assess if they are 'A' or 'B' parents. They receive a confirmation call on the day of the second lesson. This is another opportunity to get them to an 'A' and/or make up for any missed calls.

5. **They attend the second lesson.**

They are not just thrown into the lesson without any guidance (like I did back in 2004-2010). We ask parents to arrive 15 minutes before so we can do a 'second lesson meet and greet'. We don't tell them, 'Arrive 15 minutes before so we can do a meet and greet.' No, you tell them the time you want them there, and that's it. This is our opportunity to further educate the parents that we are not a club and to ask them about their self-discipline homework. We show them important things around our school, such as our self-discipline medals and sheets, success wall, and personal development books. At each point, we are using the 'assumptive' close, i.e., 'When young Bob enrols, this is where he will put his shoes and socks... When Bob enrols, this is where he will collect his attendance card... During the trial enrolment programme, these are the personal development books Bob will be covering... Can you see Bob benefiting from enrolment?' etc. We try to hold their hand so they don't feel overwhelmed. We had a good strong number of Black Belts, but the Black Belts also had to undergo Certified Instructor Training (CIT). The students who completed this became CITs. They then stood in front of the second lesson students and ensured they were not getting lost in the crowd. The CITs' job was to help the second lesson students have a great experience. The Sensei running the class also kept an eye on them and gave them positive praise and high-fives when deserved. Parents were encouraged to sit on the mats in special 'second lesson parent' chairs. You want them engaged in the experience. If you can spotlight a second lesson student for answering a question or showing great respect, or similar attitude, that will help. Only do this if it's a genuine situation where they deserve praise.

6. **They have an enrolment conference (EC) ideally on the second lesson and enrol.**

The enrolment conference was carried out at a pre-defined time before the end of the lesson. If we only had one 'A' family, the EC was at 9 minutes before the end of the lesson. The EC would again ask them about their goals and get them to confirm if they could see their child benefiting from the programme. The EC is more an art than a science. We had to cover key elements, but these key elements should have been covered in several places beforehand. Nobody had an EC if they were not showing good buying signals, if they hadn't completed the white belt self-discipline sheet, or if they were sitting there with their arms folded or constantly getting up and walking outside our school. In that case, it's not a good start. Note though that when you go into the EC

169

room, you are not selling to them. You should have created amazing value many times before then, and the selling is done from the floor. The EC is just a confirmation of goals, confirmation of which two classes they can attend, and then the price presentation. I am not going to go into detail on what is covered in the EC, but there should definitely be assumptive closes used throughout and then a price presentation with contrast sales used.

The above may seem like a lot, and I could easily spend a full day talking about the enrolment process, their experience, guestology, what you should include in both personal development packs, and much more. However, the main purpose of this book is for you to realise that your school has so much more potential.

Back in 2012-2014, I thought I was doing extremely well. I drove a nice car, had money in the bank, lived in a big house relative to my age, went on nice holidays each year, didn't have consumer debt, and my school was doing 10X, maybe even 20X, what other 'clubs' were doing. However, it was only when I really started to knuckle down on the marketing, sales, retention, and classroom format that my school took it to the next level. My mentor really helped me see the correct way forward.

I can, of course, help you with that. Just email me at hello@dervishmentoring.com.

In summary, don't think 'build it and they will come.' You need to market it, then build it, then market it again, then market it more, then market it some more. Then, you need a nailed-on enrolment process, market it, and then they will come. If you prove your true value to them, they will enrol. Never just throw a student into one of your normal lessons and hope they will enrol—that is absolute business suicide.

Now, if you are doing that and getting a good number of students to enrol (at a good price point), just imagine how much more successful your school would be with a clearly defined sales and enrolment process

Chapter 31

Price Points, Don't Compare Yourselves To Others

As I referred to earlier in this book, back in 2004, I stupidly charged less than everybody else for more. I was charging £4 for 1.5 hours when others around me were charging £4.50-£5 for 1-hour lessons! Ridiculous! Even £5 back in 2004 was too low.

I was scared to increase prices

I will hold my hands up and say that for the first 10-12 years, I was terrified to raise my prices, even by 50p. I had a scarcity mindset; I was brought up in a household where you had to treat every £1 like a prisoner because you never knew where the next one was coming from. I convinced myself that if I started to charge more, all my students would instantly leave, word would spread that I was expensive, and I would never have any more students. Stupid, I know, but maybe you can relate to something like that with your prices?

What we taught was priceless

I was foolishly comparing myself and my teaching to activities like circuit training or what the local football coach was charging. Again, I was putting myself in with seasonal recreational sports. I will say this again: I have nothing against those types of sports—football, rugby, tennis, netball—they all teach physical development and improve certain social skills. They are, however, not in the same bracket as us. Yes, we teach the physical skills of our art, but we teach so much more than that. We have a unique character development programme that teaches many transferable LIFE

SKILLS that will serve the student well throughout their life. We teach them not to give in to negative peer pressure, to set and achieve goals, to have a strong growth mindset, in addition to teaching and developing great levels of self-discipline.

If you really analyse the benefits you have gained from the years you have spent training, then you should be convinced it's had a massive positive impact on your life. The more you understand the true developmental education your lessons bring, the more you will understand how valuable it is. To my knowledge, there is no other pastime, sport, or activity that works on all the elements a true journey to Black Belt and beyond brings.

So, how much should you be charging?

This all depends on the value your programme brings. Hopefully, you are already the dearest in your area, but along with that, hopefully, you are convinced that you offer the best programme compared to others in your area, so being the dearest is justified. When we started to really professionalise our school, I slowly stepped up the price points because I was too scared to do the jump in one go (big mistake). In hindsight, I should have listened to my mentors and just done it straight away. Not listening to them was like not taking advice from an Olympic coach—crazy.

The whole reason I still invest in mentors is so they can help me become better, but for some reason, I didn't believe them on this one—a very silly decision by me. Think of it this way: Is it better to rip off the plaster slowly, then stop, then a bit more, then stop, or is it better to just pull it off all in one go? I went from charging £4 in 2004 to charging £4.50 in about 2006. Then, I introduced standing order payments in 2007, which brought the lessons back down to about £4.25. I did this to try and encourage people to pay by standing order. Foolishly, I gave them the choice. Again, in hindsight, I should have just said, 'Moving forward, we are only accepting standing order payments.'

Then, when I moved into our own full-time school, I had three price points: £36 for 2 lessons a week, £45 for 3 lessons a week (yes, only £9 more for 4 extra lessons), and £50 for unlimited. Do not offer unlimited lessons. Another stupid mistake. I was training my parents to think that the learning that took place within those 2 or 3 lessons a week was what they were paying for. I should have been charging for the outcome achieved through our programme—the numerous benefits they were receiving outside our four walls, long after our lesson had finished.

Do you remember earlier when I discussed the perceived value of your programme? I was training them to think of us as a 'cost per lesson' mentality—exactly like circuit training or football training. I hope, from reading this chapter alone, you realise that I made many mistakes in growing my business, with pricing being a big one. Ultimately, it boiled down to my confidence. I want you to speed up your school's growth by learning from me. My mentees who do the best are those that don't second-guess themselves and just follow my advice.

The £100 mental barrier

Now, in about 2017, we were charging £59 for 2 lessons a week. I thought that was quite dear, working out at about £7 - £7.50 per lesson. I was still massively undercharging. Although my confidence in my programme was growing, I still couldn't bring myself to charge the true value. In early 2018, I moved from £59 to £79. That £20 per month seemed like such a big, monumental jump. Again, my mindset was holding me back. I made the foolish mistake of asking 2-3 team members what they thought, and obviously, they thought it was too much.

Do not ask your team members how much you should charge for the programme you have designed and created. I should have just said, 'Right, from Monday, this is what we are charging,' end of discussion.

We pushed through the £100 barrier

I had to push through the £100 barrier because I knew that would be a game-changer. I still couldn't bring myself to do it, so by the end of 2018, I think we were charging £99 per month. We had, therefore, increased our prices from £59 to £99 within a year. A quick side note is that this included all gradings, seminars, licence, and membership/insurance. Don't step over pounds to pick up pennies. We don't want to have lots of negative touchpoints with money for our families.

A few months went by at this new price point, and guess what? We were still enrolling students at the same percentage as previously. I thought I would increase again by another £20, so our next price point was £119 per month. We have monetary boundaries in our heads. For instance, charging £109 or £119 is not much different because you've broken the £100 barrier.

Some instructors reading this may feel like I did years ago. You may be thinking things like:

- *'Nobody will pay that in my area.'*

- *'My competition is only ½ that price'*

- *'I live in a bad area of town.'*

- *'I've got no chance of getting students at that price.'*

- *'What about inflation?'*

- *'The government is in chaos.'*

- *'Is he crazy?'*

Trust me, I have been in your shoes. Let me tell you that in 2021, we were charging £199 per month for our programme, and students were still enrolling. Note also that this was our trial enrolment programme. For Black Belt training, it was either £299 per month or £349 per month. I'm not saying that tomorrow you can start charging that but if you work with me, we will get you there.

At reading this, you may be falling off your chair. You may even think that I'm lying, but I can 100% declare that we had over 100 members paying the above price points. If you have created the value in your programme, and it's clear to see how your school and programme teach so many transferable LIFE SKILLS, then parents will invest in your programme.

You need to clearly demonstrate that you are not just another sports club. If you create unmatched value, then parents should not try to compare you to anything else their child does. Now, this is easier said than done. Of course, you need to have a supportive, professional team, a clean and friendly school, great students, and much more, but the most important part is that your programme needs to convey to parents that this is as valuable as any other education course.

At every touchpoint, you need to demonstrate that what you are teaching is not just kicks and punches, but true character development. Don't misunderstand that. I don't want you thinking that if you have classes seven days a week and give students a free seminar every one to two weeks, you can charge whatever you want. No. This is not a case of "more is better"; it's a case of quality, not quantity. Your parents need to be bowled over by just how professional, organised, attentive, and caring your school and team are.

You need to be aware, though, that if you set your trial enrolment too low, it cripples your renewals, as the jump will be too high. Believe in your programme because if you don't, nobody else will.

In summary, like most things in life, your mindset plays a huge part. If you think you can't charge that for your programme, then you obviously don't value your programme that much, and your conversion rates will reflect that. What you are charging now is a reflection of what you think you are worth.

If you would have sat me down in 2004 and said that in 2021 you would be charging £149 per month for new students, and then they would move up to either £299 or £349 per month, I would have thought you were mad. It took me years to understand the true transformative effect our programme had on individuals of all ages. As I mentioned earlier, I would not be the person I am today, leading a comfortable life, without starting Karate. It has genuinely helped me achieve so much in my life.

Chapter 32

Negative & Positive Touch Points

Every time a prospect, student, or family member interacts with any element of your school, it is a touchpoint. Every time they look at your website, pick up the phone to call you, send an email, speak to an instructor, attend class, or enter and leave your school, it's a touchpoint. You need to look at each of those touchpoints and see how you can make it better for your clients.

Positive Touchpoints

Some examples of positive touchpoints, which may also overlap with guestology, would be:

- Answering the phone within two rings

- Being polite, as opposed to acting as if they had just gotten in the way of something important you were about to do

- Starting lessons on time

- Finishing lessons on time

- Having enough chairs for them to sit on

- Making welcome calls when they enrol

- Sending handwritten birthday cards

- Having a spotless, clean, and tidy school

- This is a big one: having clean bathrooms that have plenty of toilet paper and sanitary towels for ladies

You and your team should always assess the approach to your school and its front doors. Don't be climatized to it just because you are there most days a week.

I used to encourage my team to look for ways we could continually improve. It stemmed from our weekly meetings, where I would say, "Right – whose had a rubbish experience with a business this week?" The good thing about this was that I was training the team to look for ways we could improve (again, instructors are not just there to teach lessons). The more positive touchpoints you have, the better your business will be.

Negative Touchpoints

A negative touchpoint is any transaction (emotion or financial) that leaves a negative impression on your client. I'm not going to bullet point a list here, but a good starting point for negative touchpoints would be doing the opposite of the above positive touchpoints.

One of the worst things you can do is give your parents the feeling that every time they walk through your doors, they have to part with money. Many small clubs still operate this way, like my Sensei did 30 years ago: you sit behind a desk with a little money box and your pen, and parents line up to pay you the fee for the lesson and any other fee they need to. Please don't do this. You need to make the payment side of things automatic. The only time parents pay you is when they: 1) enrol, or 2) renew.

We all know that nothing is free (apart from air, which is good because we all need that to live), but as business owners, we need to look at collecting money as seamlessly and streamlined as possible. By doing so, you take further steps toward creating a professional learning environment, not a money-sucking machine that offers a terrible service. I say that because sometimes I go to a business and think to myself, "How is this place still so busy with this terrible service?"

Before we introduced our monthly tuition (correct terminology), here are the fees that parents would pay throughout the journey:

- Lesson fees (please do not call these 'subs')

- Grading fees (every quarter)

- Pre-grading class fee (every quarter)

- Annual membership (every year)

- Annual licence (every year)

- Fee for any seminar we offered (could be two to three times per month)

- Fee for a third lesson in a week (available every week)

- Any additional equipment they had to have throughout their programme

You may still run your school like the above, or you may have taken it one step ahead and got your students paying straight into your bank. I introduced standing order payments in about 2007-2008, but the thing with standing order payments is that if the money isn't in their account, then the standing order does not get paid, and/or they can cancel the standing order and you don't hear anything. One of the professional things we did was to work with a direct debit company who collected all our tuition on the first of the month. I would not work with this particular company again because of all the headaches of wanting to change to another provider, but they collected the money on the first, and we had it about four to five days later (they had to earn their interest as well as charging for the service). Doing this really helped with cash flow; we had all the money paid in by the 6th and all expenses paid on the 15th. Any late or missed payments, they also dealt with. We wanted to be the professional teachers who were 100% bothered about their students' development, and not the businesspeople only bothered about money.

Monthly Tuition, Not Weekly

When we introduced this, we included 99% of the above fees within the monthly tuition. The good thing about this is that your parents aren't getting a negative feeling as soon as they pull up to your school and walk through your doors (guestology). I remember mums blaming it on dads and vice versa that, when they had to bring their child to karate, it always cost them more money. Here's what was included in their monthly tuition:

- Access to two (or three) lessons per week. Do not call them lesson fees or 'subs'. Your students have a 'tuition agreement,' and you do not operate a 'pay as you play' setup.

- Grading fees (£25-£30 every 2 months, depending on grade)

- Pre-grading class fee (£7 every 2 months)

- Annual membership (£25 per year)

- Annual licence (£25 per year)

- Fee for any seminar we offered

So, before you hear silly advice from broke martial arts club owners who say they charge for X, Y, and Z, just think of it from your parents' perspective. Make it streamlined and as simple as possible.

You should not continually ask for money; just one monthly payment that covers everything is the easiest way forward. Talking about broke martial arts club owners: you need to take their technical ability off the table and assess their knowledge of running a successful and profitable business.

The 'Initial Investment'

Their initial investment is paid when they enrol, immediately after the enrolment conference. It includes everything to get them started in the trial enrolment programme. We did not say, "Well, for your suit it's £27, for your kit bag it's £7, your first licence is £25, to join is £30," etc. NO! Sometimes you'd get the "Well, he will just use his PE bag... we don't need a water bottle... How much is it for the suit only?" This was bad because then your average student value was fluctuating, and it starts to look like a mish-mash of student uniforms. This then pulls you back into the part-time club bracket. If you want to grow your school, then forget all that nonsense. Simply say, "The initial investment gets you up and running for the programme and includes everything you need for the trial enrolment programme."

Our initial investment started off at £100 but then moved to £150. Rather than tell them the price of every individual item, it's a lot easier for parents to understand that the initial investment includes everything they need for the time being. It included:

- Their suit

- Small kit bag

- Water bottle

- Progress folder (including their insurance)

- Personal development book

When you provide them with all this at the point of enrolment, they are getting tangible things that show they are a member of your school. Also, look at it from the child's point of view: when they get home and get to look at all that new 'ninja' stuff, it will be like a mini Christmas morning.

The main thing I want you to understand for this chapter is that you don't want parents thinking that every time they come to class, they need to put their hand in their wallet or purse. As a professional school owner wanting to grow a successful business, you need to be looking at EVERY element of your operation and questioning, "How can I make this better for my parents, students, and as a business operation?" Your job is to professionalise your school and not just make it look a little bit better than the club down the street, which only does two lessons a week and, regardless of grade, all students do the same class. You want to cement yourself as the most professional school in your area – the good thing is that it's not that hard to do. Engineer every part of your parents' experience, and you will notice the difference.

Chapter 33

Your Curriculum

If you are not operating a 'rotating curriculum', then your lessons are nowhere near as efficient as they could be. This, in turn, means that your students are not as good as they could be. You may not like hearing that, but it's the truth. This book is full of my confessions and mistakes as a martial arts business owner. Sticking to my old way of thinking regarding what I taught again held my progression back.

The Old-Fashioned Way

For the first 15 years of running my school, I did it the old-fashioned way. Like most of you reading this chapter, you are probably doing what your instructor taught you, right? Of course, you may have made a few minor tweaks, but nothing major. So, as a karate instructor with mixed grades in my class, I would shout to the students: "Right – white belts, you are doing reverse punch and thrust" (then I would give 2-3 quick demos). "Yellow belts, you are doing rising block, reverse punch, and thrust" (then give 2-3 quick demos). "Orange belts, you are doing step forward, face punch, body thrust" (then give 2-3 quick demos).

I would then recap again what the white belts were doing, just in case they had forgotten. I would follow that process until all the grades were doing the relevant techniques for their belts, which would include white, yellow, orange, green, blue, purple, brown, and black—at least 7 grades. Often, there were more like 10 grades because we had 2 grades for purple and 3 grades for brown belt.

To make the lessons efficient and ensure I didn't have the higher grades standing still for too long while I was explaining to the lower grades, I often got all the class doing what the white belts needed to do. Then, for the next technique, all yellow belts and above would do what yellow belts needed to do. This was good because it helped the higher grades keep on top of their lower grade techniques. I also used to get the rest of the class doing various exercises to help with their fitness until I was round to their grades.

Now, this format applied for sparring combinations, kicking combinations, katas, padwork combinations, etc. I had years of practice doing it this way, so I felt I was quite good at it. I'm sure you can relate this to your particular style. As an instructor, you need to feel the energy of the class: Are my students being challenged enough in relation to their grade? Is there too much downtime? Are my high belts not doing their techniques because they are doing lower grade techniques? Is it turning into an exercise lesson? Am I differentiating for learners?

When you introduce a rotating curriculum, your student standard will improve. All your lessons become more efficient, your students enjoy them more, and the instructor isn't spinning lots of plates. When I was a one-man band, which was for the first 10 years of my 'club', I used to teach the old-school way. When I brought in a new full-time instructor, I taught them this way too. However, as soon as we implemented a rotating curriculum, the other full-time instructors that joined the team only knew how to teach this way. Their heads would fall off if I had to tell them to teach each grade a different technique or combination in one lesson.

Applied Knowledge Is Power

The saying "knowledge is power" is great, but I believe it's not as good as it could be. It should be "applied knowledge is power." I knew about rotating curriculum probably from 2005, but I just threw it to the side and said, "I'm not doing any of that rubbish… I'm not watering down my syllabus… I'm not turning my club into a 'belt factory'." What another stupid mistake. I knew about rotating curriculum for 9-10 years before introducing it. Again, think about how much more efficient I could have made classes, which in turn would have helped student standards, which then would have helped me keep more students. I was standing in my own way again!

So please, don't overanalyse it. Just implement it from your next grading/belt testing. You can't implement it in the middle of a grading cycle.

So, How Does It Work Then?

Everybody in your lesson is doing the same thing. "What?" I hear you shout. So, my Black Belts are doing the same as my white belts? That will never work. I will explain the process and then explain how you implement it based on the size of your current (active) membership. Just remember that on your members' records, you might have 427 names, but those are members you have gained since opening your doors. However, the weekly active members you have is just 72. Don't ever kid yourself into thinking you have a large membership base because the members who left never told you they were leaving. Your active count, which is the number of students you see in a week, is the best metric for knowing your true membership base.

For each level of students, they are doing the same technique, i.e. beginner, intermediate, advanced, Black Belt.

How Do I Even Start to Do It?

You break your syllabus down into years. When I implemented my rotating curriculum, I put all the techniques, combinations, katas, padwork techniques—basically everything that students in their first year needed to cover—on an Excel spreadsheet. I then further down the spreadsheet wrote Block 1, Block 2, Block 3, Block 4.

When we first implemented the rotating curriculum, we implemented 4 blocks over a 12-month period, meaning each block was 3 months. This meant that students were testing every 3 months, which was good. But I found that this was not the ideal time frame. We then changed it to 3 blocks over a 12-month period, meaning each block was 4 months, but a striped belt grading was in the middle. This improved retention, student standards (and therefore the bottom line), because students were being tested every 2 months.

We will cover this more in the "testing" section, but every 4 months, students attempt a full colour belt, but halfway through that period, they test for a striped belt.

This is where you decide if you are going to run 4 blocks or 3 blocks over a year. We evolved into 3 blocks, where each block was a 4-month period, and it improved our school. I highly recommend to all my mentees that they adopt a 3-block period. During this 4-month period, it was full colour belt to full colour belt. However, at month 2, we had a striped belt test. Introducing striped belts into our school again helped with retention because students could see their progress quicker than I could back when I was a student.

You may have been like me—it took me 3.5 years to get to 1st Dan. I did not miss a single grading during that time, and in one of my earlier gradings, I jumped a belt because I gained very high marks across all sections (that was a good feeling). After earning my 1st Dan, I then had to wait a minimum of 2 years for 2nd, 3 years for 3rd, 4 years for 4th, etc.

Now, don't get this wrong, I am in no way at all saying you shorten the length of time between your grades—don't ruin your Dan grade timelines. You don't want a 3rd-degree Black Belt who has been training for just 3 years. What I am saying is that you need to keep testing your black belts so that they don't fall into a trap we coined 'Black Belt Syndrome'. This means that when they get to 1st degree, they say: "Well, we are just going to have a break for a few months, don't worry though, we'll be back," and then are never seen again.

It's not just you—it happened to me for the past 16-17 years of my school until we brought in an excellent Black Belt Prep cycle, which massively helped with retention of your higher grades (more on that later). Let's not forget though that for 10-20-year-old students, waiting 2 years for your next grading seems like forever.

Now, once you have written down all the curriculum you need your students to learn, you need to put the various techniques/ combinations into each block. You cannot make one block super hard and another super easy. To give you an example of what we did: we placed the hardest kata for that particular year into a block, but it was accompanied by some of the easier kicking combinations and easier basic techniques. The reason being that you do not want one block to be hard, and then as soon as they progress to the next block, it becomes way too easy.

For any Karateka reading this, there is no massive difference between Pinan Nidan, Shodan, and Sandan. Each block needs to be of similar difficulty. The question you may now have is: "Well, if each block is the same difficulty, won't each belt standard be the same?" The answer is no. As your students progress through your belts, you start to tighten the screw on their standard. So, as a brand-new white belt with a red stripe, they would not be taught the finer details of a green belt with a white stripe who is in month 10 of their programme. The higher the grade, the more technical you can be. As we both know, you can never be too good at the basics.

When you decide to implement a rotating curriculum, you should do so immediately after a grading. Ensure that the next block the students learn is the most difficult one. This ensures that your highest grades at that level, in my case, green belts in Level 1, aren't learning easier kicks, combinations, or stances when they should be progressing at their highest grades.

It all boils down to this: as long as, by the time they reach Black Belt, students have learned the syllabus you required them to learn, then what difference does it make in which order they learn it?

In summary, I understand that this concept may take some time to sink in, and you may have a lot of questions. However, I advise you to read the above again. Trust me, once you implement a rotating curriculum, you won't want to go back.

Chapter 34

Testing Aka Gradings

Grading, testing, belt testing, exams – whatever phrase you use, this is where you assess whether your students are ready for their next grade or belt. If you are following my recommended rotating curriculum format and conducting a belt test every two months (striped belts every two months, then a full colour belt on the fourth month), you will be grading roughly every eight weeks. However, you cannot say "every eight weeks" because you must allow for holidays such as Easter and Christmas, etc.

For your testing, you need to have set requirements. We all know those students – and you may have even been one of them – who didn't really need to attend every lesson, didn't try super hard, yet still received great marks and always passed their tests. Just like at school, where you are expected to attend five days a week, you need to ensure your students attend your school at least two days a week. Don't allow them to attend back-to-back lessons so that they are only attending once a week. We set a minimum of 16 lessons, equating to two lessons a week for eight weeks.

What if they miss a lesson?

Now, a question you may have is, 'Well, does this mean they can't actually miss a lesson if they want to stay on track?' A two-month period is more than eight weeks; it's closer to nine or ten weeks. Does this mean that if a student only had 14-15 lessons, they would not be eligible? Ninety percent of the time, we did allow students to grade, but it was based on their effort and progress on the self-discipline sheets, plus other factors. When students were in their trial enrolment programme or anywhere within the first 12 months, we were more flexible with their attendance. For instance, if it seemed like they were falling behind, we would organise a 1:1 lesson for 25 minutes, which equated to one normal lesson. We knew students were falling behind by reviewing attendance cards during our Monday meetings and making notes on who needed extra work.

However, don't fall into the trap of offering 1:1 lessons to everyone because some parents may think, 'Well, if I miss a lesson, I'll just get a private lesson from a Sensei, so no problem there.' That is the last thing you want them to think.

The benefit of having a set number of lessons students must attend is that it communicates to both students and parents that you have standards. This, again, is something that separates you from other 'clubs'. During a two-month grading cycle, we required a minimum of 16 lessons.

Don't burn yourself out

When I first started out, and for the first 15 years, I used to do every grading and award the belts immediately after. I would do things like not cancel any lessons because I didn't want people to call me names for cancelling, yet only a small number of students would turn up because it was their grading day. When we had an active count of over 300 students, I would hold a grading on Friday evening for advanced grades (brown belt and above), then, after four lessons on a Saturday, hold two gradings (blue and purple, yellow and orange), and then another one or two gradings on Sunday. Over the three days, I would be holding four to six gradings. I was running myself ragged. I then started travelling to other successful schools and adopting what I felt worked.

For the past three years, we have held belt tests on Saturdays and offered no scheduled lessons on that day. Depending on your school size, you may need to have two, three, or four gradings on that Saturday, followed by a graduation in the afternoon.

Why did we offer no lessons on the grading day?

Because the attendance compared to a normal Saturday was down by 80%; students tend to rest before their grading.

How did we split our gradings?

This all depends on your active count and the belts you have in your system. When we were running smoothly, we had a Level 1 (white, yellow, orange) grading, which included trial enrolment students; then we had a Level 2 (green, blue, purple) grading; then a Level 3 (brown) and above (black) grading.

Why did we not award them their belts immediately after the grading?

Because after the grading, my team and I would make final checks and cross-check everyone's belt was correct. Having students return later that afternoon was a great way to get a high percentage of your active count to attend the graduation (it's also a fantastic opportunity to highlight your Masters & Leadership programme and get member referrals).

What is a graduation?

A graduation is when students return to your school for a formal presentation of their belts, certificates, and medals. During the graduation, you award them their belts and certificates, but the most important part is where you have seating for the parents and family members of your students. During the graduation, you also have small demonstrations from select grades. We always included mini demonstrations from the youngest students, our newest yellow belts, some intermediate belts, and some Black Belts. The demonstrations from the 'red jackets' (students on our Masters & Leadership programme) were typically more advanced. They often did team kata, self-defence, or a brief weapons demonstration.

The main reason for having Masters & Leadership students was so that other students in the trial enrolment programme could look at them and think, 'I want to earn my red jacket so I can do that "cool" stuff.' The graduation separates you from other 'clubs' and further cements you as an education provider rather than just a 'seasonal recreational club'. Throughout this book, I mention the need to distinguish yourself from being categorised as just a 'sports club'; holding graduations is one of the ways to achieve this. Graduation is also an excellent opportunity to get video footage for your social media.

For the first 16-17 years (2004-2020), I did every single grading (maybe somewhere in the region of 300 gradings and perhaps 5,000 students?). I conducted every Little Ninja grading for 3-5-year-olds, as well as every striped and colour belt grading, plus every primary school grading. The only time I brought anyone in to help was for Black Belt gradings. I did this to ensure that students attending the gradings knew that an external Sensei or two would be present. That particular Sensei would not have 'student bias', meaning they would only mark based on what they saw, not whether or not the student was one of their favourites. I mention this here because if you do every single grading yourself, you are limiting your growth. You want to position yourself as the master/head/chief instructor who may attend lower gradings but who only really attends Black Belt gradings. I had competent 2nd and 3rd degree Black Belts whom I trained to handle the lower gradings.

At the end of the graduation, you would draw a line through the old curriculum block and move on to the new curriculum block. So, if your students graded on a Saturday, then the following Monday, they would begin learning new content. Just to clarify, if they had just earned their striped belt, the curriculum block would slightly change. For example, you would now teach them the rest of the kata, an additional basic technique, a padwork leg technique (because during the first block, you taught them a hand padwork technique), another sparring combination, etc. We used to provide A5 handouts to students immediately after their grading and graduation, letting them know what they would be learning the following week. We also created a brief YouTube video explaining their new curriculum. This video wasn't technical but simply a 'well done for passing your grading, this is what you're doing next' video. If they had earned a full colour belt and it was the end of the curriculum block, then we would start an entirely new curriculum on the following Monday.

Graduations Help to Highlight Who Is Close to Dropping Out

Your graduation is an ideal time to assess who is, and who isn't, earning character tabs and medals. The students who are very active are what we would class as strong students and are not that likely to drop out. The students who are not active in earning self-discipline medals are going to be very hard to renew, and they may also be close to dropping out. Following a graduation, we had a clear list of who needed to be brought back on track, and a team member was then assigned to help them moving forward. Always remember that it's easier to keep a member than to gain a new one.

To recap your grading process: you need to have set grading dates mapped out for the year ahead. Do not say the following words: "We are not holding gradings yet because I'm not happy with your progress." Imagine what this does to those students who are ready. You need to have set grading months so you can coordinate things properly. When you have a date to work towards, it forces you to make things happen. You must have a set number of lessons required by each student between each grade. You also need to cancel lessons on a Saturday (or a Sunday if you have lessons then) so that you can carry out a full day of testing and graduations.

Chapter 35

How to Run Graduations

What Are Graduations?

Graduations are when students are awarded their new belts after passing their belt test. Other awards given during the graduation might include self-discipline medals, self-discipline trophies, superstars, etc.

What Is Their Purpose?

The main objectives of the graduation are to:

- Celebrate students' success

- Have students bring a friend to watch them receive their awards

- Gather testimonials, both written and video

- Award red jackets to students who have passed their Black Belt training trial

- Present invitations to students to take part in the Black Belt training trial

Your graduations should bring your student body together to build and grow your 'Esprit de corps'.

Do not underestimate the need to tell your students that we want them to bring a witness. Don't be scared of promoting your school. Here in the UK, 95% of business owners are very scared and timid about promoting their services, and you will also notice that most businesses are really just self-employed people. I was self-employed when I started in 2004, but I grew it into a limited company as time went on. You must understand that being self-employed often means you own a job, which is a lot different from owning a systemised business. If you want to grow your school's active count and your gross revenue, you need to constantly promote it (ABM).

When Are Graduations Held?

Graduations are often held in the afternoon of the actual belt test. We held them in the afternoon, but I know other successful schools that held them the following week. They can be organised for the day after the belt test or even a week later. Holding the graduation a week later allows you more time to ensure you have every belt, medal, and trophy, and it also allows you to mop up any students who did not grade on the testing day.

If you are running your school properly, you will have been systematically reminding students of the upcoming grading and subsequently arranging make-up lessons if they are not likely to reach the minimum lesson quota. You may have also been offering a few students an intense progress lesson to raise their proficiency in weak areas of their ability. As instructors, it is our job to get students over the line by helping them. When you start to understand the need to get students to benefit from the journey to Black Belt, you will go the extra mile for them.

Your graduations should be planned for the year ahead, so they are in the diary, meaning you can plan things around them. We never informed students of the testing and graduations too far in advance because, inevitably, obstacles arise which mean plans need to be amended. One of our best live events, where we used to get +30 decent leads, was held in June, and we inevitably had to organise the testing and graduations to allow our team to get to the event. As a team, though, we knew exactly when the testing was due to take place. We could therefore announce the next graduation by handing out little reminders to parents at their current graduation. Four weeks into an 8-week cycle, we started to raise awareness and tightened up on getting students ready. In the final two weeks before the testing, we wanted everybody to be 100% clear about when their grading was, what time, and who they were bringing to the graduation. As a team, you must not forget that it is a great marketing opportunity.

Calculate Your Active Count Graduation Percentage

We wanted an absolute minimum of 90% of our active count to test. This may seem like a high percentage, but if you have 200 active students, it means that 180 are grading, and 20 are not. If you were like we were at our largest, with over 330 members, that would mean 33 members did not grade, and that is a lot of students at risk. The next step for a student not grading is to become an ex-member, so you could have 20 (or 33) potential ex-members on your hands. You will notice that members don't just leave—they drift away slowly. They miss a lesson and don't make it up. They come back, then miss a week's worth of lessons. Missing a grading is another step in that direction. For children, if they see their friends getting ahead with their belts, this is hard for them, and it ultimately takes most of them a step closer to the door. It is in your number one interest to get students ready for their gradings and to get them to take part. I've covered this elsewhere in this book, but keeping hold of a member is easier than enrolling a new one.

Team Training Before Testing

If we held school gradings on a Saturday morning, often starting at 8am, we would have finished by 1.30-2pm. The graduation was then scheduled for 3-4pm. The benefit we found from having the graduation on the same day as the belt testing was that parents were doing it all in one day, rather than spreading it over two weekends. The day before the belt testing, we often held a team training day. This also doubled up as a final check and preparation for the graduation the following day.

The team training day items and graduation prep were as follows:

- Provisionally get everybody's belts prepped

- Have their licence books open on the correct page

- Have the correct number of certificates out for the belts they were going for

- Have the invitations to apply for Black Belt training

- Coordinate which team members were gathering testimonials from which parents, and when

- Discuss the running order (e.g., new yellow belts coming up and having their belts tied by Black Belts, followed by a quick 1-minute kicking demonstration led by Sensei X; then new orange belts, who would have their belts tied by Black Belts and perform a basics (kihon) demonstration, led by Sensei Y)

- The team training day also brushed up on common questions parents asked at graduations and other Black Belt pre-framing opportunities

Perfect Opportunity to Promote Black Belt Training Benefits

Although a hectic day, especially with a large active count, it is also a great time to get the message across that training for Black Belt is key to future success in all areas of their lives. You want parents to see how the Black Belts you have produced are confident, respectful, helpful, and are also great public speakers with good foundations of leadership ability. We often had our CIT Black Belts awarding belts at the front, as well as medals. Some of the Black Belts also spoke in front of the spectators. For lots of parents, seeing 12, 13, and 14-year-old Black Belts taking part in public speaking often impresses them. For parents who haven't committed to Black Belt training, this is another positive sign that the programme works and offers great value.

Graduation Logistics

If you have a large active count, you may need to separate your graduation by relevant grades. I know schools with active counts of +400 and +500, so they had to schedule it across a weekend. For us, we split it down into the following:

- Trial enrolment and Level 1 students (white, yellow, orange)

- Level 2 students (green, blue, purple)

- Level 3 students (all brown; 3rd kyu, 2nd kyu, 1st kyu)

- Level 4 students (all Black Belts)

You have trial enrolment in with Level 1 students because you want the trial enrolment students to see other students wearing a different suit and learning different things. If you have those committed to Black Belt move straight into another class when they renew, those on trial enrolment may think they are not eligible. You want those on trial enrolment to see that people of the same, or even lower grade, can be accepted onto a Black Belt training programme. Having red jackets in your trial enrolment programme lessons is another step in the renewal process.

If you have an active count of 200 students and, for the graduation, they are only bringing one parent, that is 400 people throughout the day you could have attending your graduation. Imagine if every student brought two parents and a guest—that would mean 600 people. We did consider holding our graduation in a sports hall so we could fit them all in, but we decided against it because it was likely to cost over £350. The real reason, though, was that I thought the logistics of it all would be too much. Now, in hindsight, it would have been good to have held it in a sports hall and had all students there. It would have shown the parents and students that they are part of something big, clearly separating us from the local karate 'club'. It would also have gained interest from other people using the sports facility, and we would have gained some enquiries, which should have ended up in enrolments. That would mean you need to allocate one person to speak to these 'drop-ins' and gather their details ready for a follow-up call.

Post-Graduation Checklist

- Who was booked on but did not attend because of illness?

  o This allows us to call them on Monday to let them know about the mop-up grading taking place.

- Did we hand out invitations to Black Belt training?

  o This allows us to discuss the applicants during Monday's all-team meeting and ensure they receive the correct information at the correct time, e.g., testimonials from parents of Black Belts who highly recommend Black Belt training.

- Did everybody receive the correct belt?

- If not, whose head needs to roll? We should have minimum stock levels. If we are asking students to book in no later than one week before the grading, we should have plenty of time to order the odd belt or two.

- Did everybody receive their self-discipline awards (medals and trophies)?

  - If not then why not.

- Did we award the necessary red jackets to the relevant students?

  - If not then why not.

- Did we collect testimonials we were scheduled to collect?

  - This was a good task because it allowed team members to say they met their quota. It was also, dare I say it, a little embarrassing for team members to admit they failed their mission. Each Sensei was tasked with collecting a testimonial from a list of pre-arranged parents (the parents weren't aware).

- Is the school tidy and organised, ready for the next day?

  - This is always the case at the end of the day. A team member needs to walk around the school and check everything is as it should be, e.g., no loose pieces of paper on the mats, leftover water bottles, ample toilet rolls. Remember the saying: *'If we see it, they see it.'*

Benchmarks

By the end of a graduation, we would have a good idea of how the school did. However, more importantly, we would have precise, clear figures for the following stats:

- Percentage of students graded compared to the active count.

  For example, if we had 161 students grade but our active count was 180, that would give us an 89% graduation rate. That sounds good, but over 10% of students are at risk.

- Percentage of students who attended the level 1 grading (which is combined with the trial enrolment grading) who had committed to Black Belt training and a number who hadn't.
  For example, 12 jackets out of 24 students meant 50% of students should be renewed.

- How many invitations to apply for Black Belt training were awarded.
  This triggers the following week's process to ensure they receive more Leadership-style material, both in electronic form and tangible.

- How many students we had on trial enrolment who had not been invited but who were going to be invited within the next four weeks.

List of 'at-risk' members.

These are students who did not grade. We would then try our best to organise a mop-up grading within seven days if some students were ready to test. Even if this meant a grading of only 3-4 students, that's

3-4 students being brought back into the fold rather than stepping out of your door forever.

Why Can't I Just Give Them Their Belts After the Testing?

This was something I did from 2004 to 2017. I held the grading, parents waited outside, then they were allowed back in, and I talked about each student for about one minute each. For a grading of 30, it would take an additional 45 minutes from me talking to the first student in the front line to talking to the highest grading student in the back line. I then awarded them their belt and took a group picture.

Why did I do this? Simply because that's how my original Sensei and all the other Senseis I knew did it. Just because everybody does it doesn't mean it's the best way. Remember, *"that's the way it's always been done"* is not a suitable reason to continue doing it that way. You are reading this book because you want to professionalise your school, grow a strong cash-flowing business, and be paid well for offering a life-changing programme. So, don't copy broke club instructors. Copy and seek guidance from the successful school owners that have predictable and monthly cash flow.

You need to have all your students lined up in order of their grades. (If you are separating your graduations down, there may only be 2-3 colour grades.) You then ask them to stand up; this can be just 3-4 students or the entire group, the decision is yours. You then congratulate them, tell them their grade, and they come to the front where your CIT Black Belts remove their old belt and put on their new belt. The group then returns to their line and does a quick one-minute demonstration. It's not a demo team, it's simply a *"these are the kicks they were graded on earlier – let's see how good they all are"* type of demonstration. You then repeat the process for each grade.

Once you have completed all the grades, it's time to award them their self-discipline medals. The Senseis knew the running order and the timings because we had practised it the day before during the team training day.

Spotlight certain students, explaining that they have gone above and beyond and are showing excellent discipline. We had a quick, slick process so that when everybody who earned a Healthy Eating medal was awarded their medal, they had a group picture. Then, everybody who earned a Homework medal also had a group picture.

The best students, who were likely to stay with you for a long time, were the ones you constantly called up. They were often our highest paying members too. When you start to read books on value and price positioning, you will notice from your own member base that those who pay the most value you the most, and those who pay you the least value your service the least. (They also, within my 20+ years of school running, give you the most problems.) Do not position your school as the budget option – you are just racing to the bottom with tiny profit margins.

The demonstrations only need to be 1-2 minutes. Often, the lower the grade, the shorter the demonstration. The demonstrations could be anything relevant to your syllabus, but for us, it was:

- Board breaking

- Self-defence

- Self-defence against multiple attackers

- Kata (individual)

- Kata (team)

- Weapons

- Kicking combinations involving jumping and spinning kicks

The Black Belts needed to do something that would wow the lower grade students and parents, often self-defence against multiple attackers or some fancy-looking board breaking. You want any friends they have brought to be excited and book a lesson.

Numerous times throughout the grading, Senseis should be giving the guests clear instructions on who to speak to and where they are located to book their first lesson. If you don't have instructors, then these can be well-trained CIT members or evangelical parents who adore your programme. A prospect in your school should not be left thinking about who they need to speak to about booking a first lesson. It needs to be crystal clear what they need to do; there needs to be a simple call to action.

In summary, the graduations are a great way of keeping students on track, which in turn means having a stable, cash-flowing business. The above are my humble thoughts on how a graduation should be run. You can, of course, modify it for your school, but what you must remember is that it is there to celebrate your students' success, which in turn helps retention. Graduations are also a fantastic way to get trial enrolment students excited about the prospect of becoming a Black Belt and for the Black Belts to demonstrate their skills.

Chapter 36

Retention; Tips, Tools & Strategies

Retention of your students is crucial to growing your school. Remember what I said at the start of this book—you need to enrol and keep a student forever. If you can do that, you will be successful.

You must view retention as being just as important as marketing. In fact, you could argue that it is even more important because there is no point in investing heavily in marketing (whether in money, time, or a combination of both) if students leave within a short period. Your school should not have a revolving-door culture.

We experienced a revolving door for a good few years, but because I didn't track the numbers, I didn't realise it. I simply assumed that because class sizes were consistently high, the business was doing well. As I mentioned in the stats chapter, we need to fill all the holes in our bucket if we want to grow a profitable business.

For several years, when we reviewed our end-of-year stats, we discovered that we were enrolling an average of 10 students a month, but 8.5 of them were leaving within their first 12 months. That means we enrolled 120 students in a year, but only 18 remained the following year. That level of dropout is unsustainable. At that rate, it would take nearly six years to achieve a net enrolment of 100 students. I know schools that have gained 100 students in just two months. Our personal best was about 37 in one month and around 75 in a quarter.

Yes, I thought we were doing well because our classes were always full, we were still enrolling members every month, and we were making money—have you ever said those things? When you start to look deeper, you realise that while you are enrolling students, they are coming in the front door and quickly leaving through the back. Your monthly gross slowly creeps up, and when you compare January to December, your revenue has grown, but often not in line with inflation. This means you're essentially in the same position as 12 months ago. Your school needs to experience consistent growth each month, quarter, and year. My goal for my mentees is to consistently grow their school and profits.

Improving Retention

Solving your retention problem will enhance the student experience because they will benefit from the training you promised them when they enrolled. One of my mentors put it this way: *We are doing them a disservice if they don't stay long enough to improve their lives.*

Yes, having long-term students is good for your bottom line, but more importantly, it's fantastic for them. You must believe in your programme and that the longer students stay, the more their lives will improve. I mention this elsewhere in the book, but it makes me shiver when I think of the thousands of students I enrolled who left before they had the chance to develop any meaningful, transferable LIFE SKILLS. I don't want that to happen to you.

What Is Retention?

If you're unsure what we mean by retention, it simply refers to the number of students you keep each month, quarter, or year. At our best, we had a retention rate of about 2.6%. We typically hovered around 3–4%, which, while not amazing, was significantly better than a typical 'club.'

Like most strategies in this book, the more you implement, the better your school will become. As mentioned in *Atomic Habits* (another one of our Black Belt training books), *you can't improve one thing by 1,000%, but you can improve 1,000 things by 1%.* Just introduce one or two new strategies per week, and before you know it, your school will be in a much better position.

I help my mentees achieve significant results within six weeks of working with me—their net enrolment increases, and so does their bottom line.

Strategies to Improve Retention

Just as with marketing, there isn't one single tool or strategy that will gain you 100 members in a week. Retention works the same way—it isn't just one thing that keeps students enrolled; it's a combination of many factors.

One of my greatest mentors always said that renewing students is one of the best retention tools out there, along with building a genuine rapport with and concern for your student body. I 100% agree with that.

Here are some of the things we implemented to improve retention:

- **Award A5 certificates at the end of every class.**

  We always had a *Star of the Class* certificate, but we also awarded others depending on class size, such as *Best Beginner*, *Excellent Potential*, and *Good Job*. These were not participation certificates—if no one deserved it, we didn't award one. See Bonus Section 4 for a sample.

- **Award character tabs for students completing their self-discipline sheets.**

  These should be awarded at the front of the class during the final few minutes. Character tabs are attached to the student's belt and serve as a visible indicator of engagement. A lack of engagement is a strong predictor of dropout.

- **Spotlight students before, during, and at the end of a lesson.**

Allowing students to showcase their skills boosts their confidence and makes them feel special. It also pleases parents when they see their child's efforts being recognised. Students can either demonstrate techniques in line or at the front of the class.

- **Handwrite 'Awesome Letters.'**

At the end of each day, we wrote letters to two or three students (depending on class size and active student count). Never underestimate the impact of a handwritten letter in a handwritten envelope—it shows you've gone the extra mile. It has far more impact than an email or text.

- **Make 'Happy Birthday' calls on students' birthdays.**

Self-explanatory.

- **Write 'Happy Birthday' cards.**

All team members signed them, often adding a doodle or a note about setting goals.

- **Send 'Get Well Soon' cards.**

If we found out that any student or their immediate family (including parents or grandparents who often attended class) was ill, we sent a card.

- **Send handwritten 'Merry Christmas' cards.**

   Never use a print shop for this. Always handwrite them. We started writing our Christmas cards right after Halloween. When I drove a nice, expensive car, I often received mass-printed Christmas cards from the car garage—they never gave me the *aww, they really thought about me* feeling.

- **Welcome parents and students as soon as they walk through our doors.**

   Self-explanatory.

Systemising Retention

We had all of the above systemised. Every Monday during our team meeting, we reviewed upcoming birthdays and wrote cards. We also went through our entire member base to see if anyone had relevant updates about students or their families.

With a team of eight staff, our all-team Monday meeting was crucial for identifying gaps. When you start doing this, you'll be surprised by how often you hear things like, *Oh, I forgot to tell you...* or *I thought you already knew.* You'll also realise that some team members assume everyone else knows something when, in reality, they don't.

Never assume your entire team knows everything—always verify.

Keeping Your Team Informed

Another important part of these meetings was reviewing our stats. Your team needs to understand exactly how the school is performing. If you don't share your stats, how can they know if they're doing well? By default, they'll assume they're doing a great job simply because they're showing up on time, working, and going home. But team members need real feedback. If I were underperforming, I'd want to know—especially if I mistakenly thought I was excelling.

The Bigger Picture

By now, I'm sure you understand—you need to have a genuine concern for your students. We want them to lead a life where martial arts training is a key foundation. Think about how much martial arts has shaped your life.

If you could go back in time to the moment you first stepped onto the mats, would you do it all over again?

Your goal is to convey to your students the benefits you've experienced through consistent martial arts training. This is especially important during the enrolment and renewal process. We need to explain the transferable LIFE SKILLS they will develop— not just their improved fitness levels.

How Do You Track Retention?

We used to have a daily stats email sent every day, and as part of that email, it included the number of enrolments and the number of ex-members. The team then calculated the net enrolment. It's a simple equation:

How many members we enrolled – How many members we lost.

This then fed into the end-of-week (EOW) stats, which, in turn, fed into the end-of-month EOM stats. All stats were covered in the all-team meeting on Monday. I never wanted to use the red marker on the flip chart because it meant that we had lost a member. The colour coding of your flip chart stats table makes things stand out even more. Red meant an ex-member, green meant a new enrolment or renewal.

During our end-of-month meeting, we would have a clear figure of our net enrolment. On a side note, this could NEVER be a negative number! If we did have a negative number, then the following month's marketing plan was increased to make up for that month's poor performance. The end-of-month meeting was also recorded because it explained how the team were going to improve for the next month. This footage would then be watched during the all-team meetings the following week. You want to build a team that is accountable. They can't just get bonuses when the school is doing well and nothing happens when performance is slipping. It's not the Premier League.

Working Out Your Retention

To work out your retention, you do the following calculation:

Number of lost members this month

Divided by

Active count

So, if we had lost 5 members and our active count was 100, it would be:

$5 \div 100 = 0.05 = 5\%$ (that needs work).

If we had lost 3 but our active count was 300, it would be:

$3 \div 300 = 0.01 = 1\%$ (amazing).

It was always more accurate to calculate our retention every quarter, then every 6 months, and the best figure was for the whole year. The bigger the time frame you look at, the more accurate your retention figure would be, simply because it can skew easily across a month. Your best performance metrics are comparing YTD (Year to Date) and then comparing each year to the previous one.

I suggest you track your retention figure for the previous month. If you have figures for the previous 3-6 months, then great. Now, when you start to implement some of the strategies in this book, make a clear mark so you know if they are having an effect (which they will).

Never be complacent and think you have it nailed. We knew that if, in one month, we didn't lose any members, then the following month, we were going to lose more than usual. This balanced it out.

Don't Be Cheap

So many martial arts instructors don't like to spend money. Not you, though, because you bought this book. So many instructors would have scoffed at the price, but those same instructors are the ones who will never grow. They are the ones who think, "I'm a great instructor; students will automatically enrol." Wrong! They seem to forget that you need to continually invest in your business. You cannot just take, take, take. If I had spent £250 to get a member (which, by the way, I would do all day long because I know how valuable a member is to my school), then I will spend some money to keep hold of them. Make calls to check on them, send them "We're missing you in class" cards, make home visits, etc. It is easier to keep a member than to gain a new one.

When my mentees ask me, "What's the best way to keep hold of students?" it's not just one thing. It's a series of often small things that all contribute. If I were to say what is the best way, it would have to be renewing your students to Black Belt—not a flaky renewal, a proper one. I mean one where parents see the true value a Black Belt journey brings.

In summary, retention is a huge part of your school's growth. Marketing becomes pointless if you can't keep hold of students long enough.

Dervish Dervish

Chapter 37

Terminology; Good and Bad

The Use of Language

The language you and your team use separates you from a 'club'. Correct terminology places you in a professional, educational environment. The language and terminology you use, like most aspects of this book, are not the only factors that help your school become more professional. However, when combined with elements such as guestology, positive touchpoints, an excellent learning environment, and sincere team members, they all contribute to making you stand out.

Pronounce Your T's and G's

Let me say this right away—I am in no way a Shakespearean actor, nor have I ever taken part in regular (if any) elocution lessons. I will be the first to admit that I do not speak eloquently. However, you and your team must make an effort to pronounce your T's and G's.

During team training, you should encourage your staff to listen carefully to how they pronounce their 'T' and 'G' sounds in certain words. Are they slipping into slang, as if they're chatting with friends down the pub? As a karate instructor, it used to frustrate me when I heard phrases like:

- "Rite, we are gona do some ka-uh now."

  - It should have been: "RighT, everybody, we are goinG to do some kaTa now."

- "Get ya sparin gloves on – we're gona do some sparin."

- It should have been: "OK, go and put your sparrinG equipment on. We are all going to do some sparrinG."

- "Yer kidin aren't ya?"

  - It should have been: "You are kidding, aren't you?"

I won't write any more examples—I'm sure you get the idea. From now on, you'll probably find yourself paying closer attention to how people speak.

If you scroll through any of my YouTube videos or work with me directly, you'll see that I am in no way perfect, nor do I claim to be. Interestingly, it was not the older team members who tended to fall into this habit—it was often the younger ones.

For those who have never heard me speak, let me assure you: I have never taken elocution lessons, nor do I sound like someone who studied English Literature at Oxford or Cambridge. However, when I was building my school, it was my job to ensure my team raised the bar so that the value we provided was worth far more than what we charged per month. The value you provide must always far outweigh the cost your students' parents are paying.

Greetings

Whenever anyone walks into your school, they need to be acknowledged within three seconds. If it's their first visit and, for some reason, they haven't been greeted at the door—for example, if they are a 'drop-in' (an enquiry that didn't contact you beforehand and just turned up)—they must still be acknowledged within three seconds.

I'm not saying you should drop everything and sprint over to them, but they need some form of recognition. This could be as simple as:

- Eye contact and a smile

- A quick "Hello" with a gesture indicating you'll be with them soon

- A thumbs-up or raising your index finger to signal "One minute"

I know I keep mentioning "your team", but I was a one-man band for the first ten years, so I understand how challenging this can be during class. However, you must train yourself to always be aware of your front door.

If your entrance is along one wall of the building, position your class so their backs face the door while you keep it in view. If that's not possible, ensure that when you stand at the front, you are the closest to the door. Every part of your school should be engineered for success.

You only have one chance to make a first impression—it had better be a good one. One of the worst things you can do is ignore people when they walk in. Do so at your peril.

Conversations

Your team should never discuss wild parties they've attended (or are planning to attend). Likewise, you don't want them talking about their "mad friend" who always gets drunk and causes trouble.

Your instructors should not give one-word answers, but they must also be aware of what they talk about, as this will shape (rightly or wrongly) the image of your school. As a parent, ask yourself: do you want one of your child's role models (because, for many younger students, a martial arts instructor is just that) to be someone who parties all weekend, speaks casually, turns up to work late, lacks focus, or has poor hygiene?

I could exaggerate the example further, but the point remains: you and your instructors must be professional at all times. This links back to Disney's *Guestology*.

Of course, you can't dictate who your team socialises with outside work. However, if they are serious about building the business and brand, they should be mindful of the image they present.

During their induction, or even if they're just teenagers assisting with lessons, you should provide guidance on best practices for social media. Parents might send friend requests to you or your team members, and if they see content that doesn't match your school's professional image, it could harm your reputation. As a school owner, you need to stage-manage as much as possible.

On a personal level, I was never on Facebook, but if I had been, I wouldn't have accepted friend requests unless my profile was 100% tailored to enhance my business.

Sales Language

The language used in any sales environment can influence the success of the sale—or in our case, an enrolment or renewal.

You never want to come across as a sleazy used car salesman. Yes, I know there are plenty of honest, brilliant used car salesmen out there, but for this example, picture someone trying to sell you a terrible car at an extortionate price while taking your last penny.

Do not use the following words:

- Contract

- Sign

- Deposit/Set-up fee

Instead, use:

- Tuition agreement (NOT contract)

- Scribble here or initial here (NOT sign)

- Initial investment (NOT deposit/set-up fee/registration fee)

I could go into much more detail about good and bad terminology, but my aim in this book is to highlight just how much attention to detail you should be paying when running your school.

The best athletes in the world are meticulous in their approach. To become more successful, you must focus on the details. However, don't let yourself fall into 'analysis paralysis'. Prioritise the big things first—the actions that will move your school forward the fastest. That means marketing your school effectively and retaining students for longer.

There are thousands of sales books available, and I've read a fair few. One of the best is *How to Master the Art of Selling* by Tom Hopkins. While it's aimed at full-time salespeople, even picking up five or six best-practice ideas from the book can positively impact your school's success.

I've mentioned *Guestology* in this book, and if you're serious about growing your business, I recommend researching it further. Start by implementing small changes—aim for just one per week over the next few weeks. These small improvements will compound over time, enhancing both your school's professionalism and its growth.

Chapter 38

A Great Trial Enrolment Lesson

Your marketing is designed to get them to make contact with you. Your enquiry checklists and scripts are designed to get them through your front doors. Your first lesson is designed to create value in your programme and to get them to return for a second lesson. Your second lesson is designed to enrol a student.

Your marketing could have been designed by one of the best marketing agencies in the world, and your intro lesson could be delivered by the most successful school owner in the country, but if your second lesson doesn't live up to their expectations, then you won't be enrolling anybody.

If you have followed the process outlined in this book, then you will have delivered an amazing first lesson (consultation), and your student and their family will be very excited to return to your school. They are coming back with the intention of enrolling if they like what they see. Their mindset is: *If we like today's lesson, we will enrol.*

When you have enrolled a student, though, your job is only just beginning. Once they have parted with their money, you now need to earn it.

The Second Lesson

The second lesson is not a private lesson; they are taking part in a trial enrolment lesson with other students. You are not just throwing them into a class, though. Like all elements of your school, you will have stage-managed it well, and you or your team will know exactly what to do and when to do it.

Basic Points for a Trial Enrolment Lesson:

- It needs to be the right combination of learning and fun.

- They need to be looked after by a CIT (and the lead Sensei).

- Spotlight them.

- They should be awarded their white belt in front of the class.

- You need to cover the major elements of what was covered in the intro lesson, plus more.

- The lesson needs to start and end on time.

- Skills drill if deserved at the end.

Creating Value in the Lesson:

- A success quote needs to be covered.

- A chapter of the week should be covered in your personal development chat.

- Woven throughout the lesson should be the need for respect and focus at home and in their classroom. (Only writing one sentence here actually undersells how important this is.)

Making a Lasting Impression

Your parents need to feel the friendly atmosphere of your school. One way to achieve this is to have Black Belts introduce themselves to the students. The Black Belts also need to introduce themselves to the parents, saying something like:

"Hi, nice to meet you both. My name is X, and I will be looking after Bob today."

Your Black Belts, or whoever you assign to help your second lesson students, need to be *a product of the product*—they should behave exactly as you want them to.

Throughout the lesson, the parent support group needs to be convinced that what you are teaching cannot be provided elsewhere. If you just turn it into an exercise class, then your chances of enrolling them are slim.

You and your instructors need to glance over at the parents during the lesson and ensure they have a big smile on their faces.

Logistics

During your quick team meeting earlier in the day, you should have already worked out:

- Who is doing the warm-up.

- Who is doing the second lesson meet-and-greet.

- Who is doing the EC and at what time.

You are likely to know which CIT students are in attendance because of the CIT timetable you have.

As soon as you increase your marketing, you should notice an increase in leads, which means you will be getting more practice with the second lesson process. Each second lesson should aim to be smoother and more efficient than the previous one.

Selling from the Floor

This is a huge part of your enrolment puzzle. You or your instructor needs to demonstrate how training with you will help them in their classroom and at home. In fact, your training will help them *everywhere.*

The enrolment conference is not where you hoodwink them into enrolling; it is where they finalise the details because they are already happy with what they have seen so far.

The instructor should be saying things like:

- *"Now remember, it's no good showing respect here—you need to show it..." (students answer).*

- *"We have gone over the student creed, but what does self-discipline actually mean...?"*

- *"Our success quote is 'Fall down seven times, get up eight.' I think that means determination and perseverance. Who here can tell me when they showed perseverance?"*

- *"If you can show me focus here, then you should be showing focus in your classroom too. Has anybody shown focus today at school or at home?"*

- *"Put your hand up if you are going to do some of these small daily disciplines we have been talking about."*

- *"Everybody, a Black Belt is not just here (pointing to your belt); it is your mindset. It is here (pointing to your head)."*

- *"When you commit to becoming a Black Belt, I know that you will start to do better in all areas of your life. That's what we want, and that's what your parents want. Let's be the best we can be, everybody."*

We had three pages of Selling from the Floor (SFF) quotes that team members needed to learn. They were separated into *easy, medium,* and *hard.* The difference between each level was how long the sentence or paragraph was.

What Happens if They Are Not Ready to Enrol?

A third lesson should be booked when they are first seated for their 2nd lesson. We do this so that, just in case you do not get around to speaking to them, you have already scheduled their third lesson.

This should *only* ever happen, though, if you are overbooked with second lessons and they are all 'A'-rated.

Having a third lesson booked reduces the chance of people falling through the cracks.

The quality of an instructor was based not on their technical skill, but on their ability to motivate people to learn more and become the best they wanted to be.

I'm sure from reading the above, you get the idea.

On their second lesson at your school, it is not your job to make them technically better—after all, what's the point if they don't enrol? Your role is to make them think:

"Wow, this is amazing—why have we not enrolled sooner?"

In summary, your job during that second lesson is to enrol a new student. You can only do that by providing a great experience where the transferable LIFE SKILLS you teach are clear to see from your parents' perspective.

Chapter 39

What Do You Do When You Get An Ex-Member?

As a serious business owner, you need to constantly layer on retention systems while increasing the value of your programme. Unfortunately, you do lose members. As I've mentioned throughout this book, it's your job to plug the holes in your bucket so that as few members are lost as possible.

I remember reading a book about membership models where the author took a cynical approach. He said that as soon as you enrol a member, you have lost a prospect, and they are now just on the road to dropping off. Yes, it is a cynical viewpoint, but I can understand where he is coming from. I definitely agree that as soon as you enrol a member, your best prospect has gone, meaning they need replacing—this is why you must constantly be marketing. Always Be Marketing (ABM).

As soon as you take your foot off the pedal with marketing, your school starts to die. Reducing your marketing efforts is a sure way to decline.

The Dreaded Email

When you receive the email (or very occasionally a phone call) letting you know that a member is not coming back, you must call them. You follow the 'just got an ex-member' script and find out why they have decided to stop.

It might be one of the classic lines: *'They just don't want to come anymore, and I don't want to drag them.'* This again is down to framing your programme properly. Parents need to see your school and its teaching as a crucial part of their child's development.

During team training, I always used to give this example: if my children ever said, *'Dad, I don't want to go to school anymore,'* I would say, *'I understand, but you're still going.'* Not that I 100% agree with what the formal education system teaches, but I know that—apart from it being illegal not to send them—school is great for their development.

I doubt you can create the same level of emphasis as the school system with your martial arts programme, but at every stage, you must add value so that parents see the LIFE SKILLS their children are learning.

You may even get the *'They just want to try something else'* line. Again, this may or may not be the actual reason. Regardless, you need to take some ownership—if they no longer enjoy your lessons or see value in them, that's on you. Lessons should be challenging, educational, and fun.

If they want to try something else, great. They have five other days in the week to choose from. If your programme were truly valuable, the parents would be saying, *'Yes, you can try something else, but you're not stopping karate.'*

It all comes down to educating them on the true value of your programme. The journey to Black Belt and beyond is incomparable to anything else. Just as you should always be marketing for new members, you must also market for renewals and provide parents with plenty of social proof about the endless benefits of training to Black Belt with you.

Keeping in Touch with Ex-Members

If we couldn't re-engage them, their details went onto a 'reactivation' list. We never wanted our families to forget about us completely. Remember the saying: *'Out of sight, out of mind.'* We did not want that to be us.

Some things we used to do:

- Send them birthday cards (1 per year)

- Send them Christmas cards (1 per year)

- Send them Happy Easter cards (1 per year)

- Send them Happy New Year cards (1 per year)

- Invite them to events at your school (1 per month = 12 per year)

- Offer a FREE month of tuition (6 per year)

- Send them Black Belt graduation pictures and write-ups (2 per year)

The general theme is—keep in touch with them! Let them know that you and your students are doing great things. Whatever method you choose, you want them to see you and your school regularly.

I'm not talking about contacting them daily, but ideally, they should receive an email from you once a week or fortnight and physical mail every 1–2 months. You can send them invitations to events, which could include a FREE month of training.

Please don't step over pounds to pick up pennies. Don't be afraid to spend money on stamps and send them information. I know so many instructors who won't do anything to try to get ex-members back. If you're reading this book, then I expect you're not in that camp— you're in the *building a profitable martial arts school* camp.

Why Bother Trying to Get Them Back?

It's easier to re-engage an ex-member than it is to convince a prospect to enrol in your school. The easiest sale you will ever make is the second sale to the same person. You already have rapport, and they have previously bought from you.

The hesitancy you might experience during an initial enrolment is often non-existent or significantly lower when they re-enrol. When an ex-member walks back through your doors, the re-enrolment often happens the same day.

Just like a brand-new member, do not just throw them into class. We used to organise 1–2 private lessons to bring them back up to speed. You don't want them to have left as a purple or brown belt, then get back into class and realise their fitness, standard, and flexibility have deteriorated. That can be a blow to their self-esteem.

If you organise 1–2 private lessons (or as many as they need), it will help with the transition. Plus, it shows the parents that you care about the student. Give them a FREE suit—make them feel valued and glad to be back.

Do not penny-pinch. If your suits cost £25–£35 trade, wouldn't you be happy spending that to get a member back into your system? What a great return on investment—£35, and you've just gained a new member who will soon be paying tuition again.

The Numbers Game

When you start tracking your stats, you can calculate how much an enrolment costs you per month (*amount spent on advertising ÷ number of enrolments = cost per enrolment*). The longer you track your stats, the better your understanding of this figure.

Once you've been tracking for a year, you'll have a solid baseline. If this amount is £500, then ask yourself: *'Is it worth spending £500 to get a new member, or should I spend a fraction of that to get an old member back in the system?'*

The answer, of course, is to do both—but you must actively try to re-engage old members.

Not Every Member is Worth Retaining

Let me be clear—I'm fully aware that some members you won't want back. In fact, there are some you'll be glad to see leave.

You'll find that once you realise the true value of your programme and start charging more, it's usually the ones who pay the least that give you the most headaches.

We had members paying £350 per month (for a single student), whose parents were amazing and couldn't praise our programme enough. Then we had some old members who enrolled at £59 per month and were constantly unhappy. They would sit in the school with their arms folded and a scowl on their face. I was always pleased when these left.

That was our fault—we hadn't framed the true value of the programme when they enrolled. In their minds, it was only worth £59 per month. We had positioned ourselves in the *seasonal, recreational sport* bracket—a big mistake if you're trying to grow your school.

In summary, you must not just forget about your ex-members. It's easier to re-enrol an old student than to gain a new one. Keep in touch with them—they might re-enrol or even refer friends to your friendly and professional school.

Chapter 40

Systems & Standardisation

If you are looking to seriously grow your school (which I assume you are, otherwise you've picked up the wrong book), you need to have systems for everything. Depending on your business growth knowledge, you may or may not have come across the famous book on systems called *The E-Myth* by Michael E. Gerber.

I first read this in about 2007 and was very excited that I could train somebody up to do things just as well as I could. The only problem was that I had nobody to train. I had no adult members. I didn't even think about the 10-year-old students and above—I assumed nobody below first-degree Black Belt could be trained, and definitely nobody under 18 years old. With that type of thinking, I was already ostracising about 98% of my members.

As instructors and businesspeople, we need to learn to get out of our own way sometimes. I had students, which meant I could have introduced systems training.

What is a system?

Rather than overcomplicating things, a system is basically a set of instructions—steps, if you like—that are carried out to ensure a process is done properly.

We all have systems in our everyday life; we just don't write them down. You probably wake up at the same time, have breakfast at the same time and in the same place, brush your teeth the same way, take the dog on the same route, set off to work at the same time, etc. Your life is full of systems—they're just not documented.

It's your job as a business owner to write them down.

Look at it this way—if you get knocked over by a bus tomorrow, does your business still run? I know that mine did not run 95% on its own until about 2018.

If you can see how you are limiting your school's growth, then please pay attention to this chapter.

The most important systems to grow your school

The key systems you need are:

- A marketing plan

- How to deal with an enquiry (drop-in, call, email, Facebook, text)

- How to 'meet and greet' for consultation/intro 1

- Delivery of intro 1

- How to 'meet and greet' for the second lesson

- Delivery of the second lesson

- How to 'sell from the floor'

- Enrolment conference

- Progress folder conference

- Black belt pre-framing (on the mats, off the mats)

- Renewal conference

The more members we gained and the more we educated ourselves, the more systems we created.

However, for those of you who know many of Bruce Lee's quotes, remind yourself of the one regarding 'simplicity'. As school owners, we should not aim to make things complex. Our goal with systems is to make them as simple as possible while still achieving the desired outcome.

One of the huge advantages of the iPhone when it was first released was that it could be operated by a five-year-old. Apple made the user experience incredibly simple. Your systems need to be just as easy to follow.

Training your team on systems

In your weekly team training, you should always cover and train on the main systems of your business, then rotate through the less important or less frequent ones each week.

During a typical eight-week grading cycle, we would cover our core eight systems. The core systems are the ones that have the biggest impact: selling from the floor, consultation delivery, enrolment conference, etc.

If I realised that some core systems were not as strong as they should be, I would organise an extra team training session that week. Just remember, we are only as strong as our weakest link.

You will know if some systems are lagging by looking at your crucial stats. If you are getting plenty of leads and getting them through the door but not back for the second lesson, the stats will reflect that. This should then draw your attention to your intro delivery.

Teaching and floor management systems

Here are some systems specifically related to teaching and floor management:

- Your positioning, body language, and tonality

- What warm-ups are done (and when)

- How long personal development chats should be (and when to have them)

- How to spotlight students (and when)

- When and how to award the white belt to the second-lesson student

- Self-discipline speech, including awarding character tabs

- Awarding certificates

- What to do if a student is late

- Where attendance cards go once collected

Avoiding burnout and ensuring longevity

If you are like I was between 2004 and 2012, then you do absolutely everything—you are the head chef and chief dishwasher.

I didn't mind doing everything… until I did mind doing everything.

If you can see yourself teaching for the rest of your life, then excellent—your students will greatly benefit from your knowledge. But you must also think about the day you might not enjoy teaching as much as you do now—what happens then?

When I left my lecturing job and went full-time into building the school, I can honestly say I loved it.

You need to make sure you have systems for the biggest components of your business and then train people up on them.

Don't be naive, like I was when I first started growing a team, and assume that because you have trained someone once, they will never get it wrong or forget it.

Treat your systems training like your martial arts training—you need to constantly practise, practise, practise, and then practise some more. The more you train, the more you will want your team to pick up the finer details.

Think of it like pad work—it's easy to get a student to strike a pad at about 80% of their potential. You then continually polish, tweak, and refine the movement until they are near 99% potential.

The same goes for your systems. Train someone until they are at least 70% as good as you, then let them take over. However, you must supervise the system—don't just assume everything will run smoothly without your oversight from time to time.

How often should you train your team

At least once a week. We used to hold an all-team meeting every Monday, during which we reviewed the past seven days' stats and assessed our progress from a YTD (year-to-date) perspective—i.e., were we performing better or worse than the same time last year?

The meeting lasted approximately two hours (always have a clear start and finish time; otherwise, meetings can easily drag on too long). The first 45–50 minutes were dedicated to reviewing stats and confirming marketing tasks for the next 1–3 weeks. The remainder of the meeting focused on training for one of the core systems. Regardless of how experienced a team member was, everyone participated in this weekly training.

Since we worked extensively in primary schools, we also held a team training day once per term—i.e., every six weeks. This was an intensive training session focused on the company's direction and strengthening weaker systems.

The day before a grading and graduation, we organised an all-team training day to prepare belts, self-discipline medals, trophies, superstars, and Black Belt training invitations for the following day. This session also included additional training on areas I felt needed improvement across the team. As with all our sessions, both training slots had clear start and finish times, along with a structured agenda.

If a particular team member struggled with a system, we organised targeted, intensive training—typically 45-minute sessions, two to three times per week, for two to three weeks. This usually brought them up to a reasonable level. They may not become perfect, but it is your job to get them to at least 70% as good as you.

For those who admire the greatest athletes of all time, remember that they excel because they dedicate relentless hours to the fundamentals, even when no one is watching. The same principle applies to your team—success is built through repetition and refinement.

Build from Within

One of the great advantages of developing your instructors from within is that you can shape and mould them from day one. Start with small tasks—such as teaching them how to sweep up properly—before progressing to higher standards of cleanliness and, eventually, lesson systems. Once they become full-time instructors, you can train them on more advanced systems like enrolment conferences and consultations.

Regarding cleaning duties, you don't want a Black Belt dismissing the task as beneath them. We reminded our students that in Japan, all students are responsible for maintaining the cleanliness of their dojo as a sign of respect and humility. I never minded cleaning the toilets because I believed it demonstrated to both my team and students that if the Master Instructor could do it, so could they.

What Not to Do

Never put a team member on the spot by saying, *"Right, you're doing the warm-up in two minutes."* While confident students might rise to the occasion, experience tells me that these warm-ups often resemble generic P.E. sessions—too intense and lacking clear differentiation between grades.

Instead, focus on developing their *style* while ensuring their warm-ups align with your school's energy and dynamics. My recommendation is to record 3–5 of your own warm-ups and have them compare the similarities. Watch the recordings beforehand and make a list of key points you want them to notice.

They will realise that you repeat the same phrases, use the same tone, and maintain the same body positioning and language consistently. Instruct them to watch *you* rather than the students. This exercise not only helps them refine their technique but also highlights areas where you need to improve.

In summary, training your team on systems is an ongoing process—it is never complete. Yes, you can train them to a certain level, but without continuous reinforcement, bad habits will creep in. Regular, structured training ensures consistency and keeps your school running at its best.

Part 6
BLACK BELTS AND INSTRUCTORS

Chapter 41

Black Belt Retention

If your school is still in its early days and your highest-grade students have only been with you for two years or less, then do not spend any time planning your Black Belt preparation or Black Belt grading. If I had opened my school and my highest grades at the moment were nowhere near Black Belt, I would not be looking at this section in great depth until they were close. However, if you have been running your school for a number of years and have held Black Belt gradings, then this section should provide you with some useful ideas on how to help your Black Belts stick around longer.

It's All in the Conditioning (aka Framing)

If you have pre-framed your students from day one and carried out the renewal process properly, then the number of students staying past years one, two, and three will dramatically improve. Remember that renewing students is a huge key to retention.

I remember in 2008 when I held my first-ever Dan grading—I had just five students attend (this was still when I was doing so many things wrong). One of our biggest Dan gradings had over 30 students. Although this was a lot better and looked like a scene from *Enter the Dragon*, I could still see so many holes in my operation that needed to be plugged.

An outsider looking in might see the Black Belt grade as being a complete master of their art, but as an instructor, you know this is far from the case. Earning a Black Belt shows that you have learned the basics. I am currently a 6th Dan Black Belt, and I still consider myself an absolute beginner—I still have so much to learn. You probably feel the same.

Keeping Hold of Black Belts

For the first 8–10 years of running Dan gradings, I tried so many things to keep students around once they had earned their grade. The problem was that I was listening to people who didn't run successful schools. Never listen to people who are less successful than you are.

They told me to do things like:

- Hold special Black Belt-only classes

- Give them a special Black Belt patch

- Have them wear a new suit

- Plus much more

Now, the point to remember here is that all these are *okay* suggestions. They're not terrible, and some of them will contribute to retention. However, what these instructors were missing was that whatever got students to Black Belt will keep them going as Black Belts.

When I passed my 1st Dan in 2000, I had to wait a minimum of two years before attempting 2nd Dan (2002), then a minimum of three years before going for 3rd Dan (2005), and so on. It may be the same in your style. The long and short of it is that we need to keep our students progressing. They need to feel that they are still moving forward.

I want to be clear—I am not saying you should lower your standards. Not at all. But you do need to keep students motivated and progressing.

We still had students test every two months, meaning that from 1st to 2nd Dan, there were 12 tests over the 24-month period. After each test, students earned something for their belt. To avoid having them do small 1.5–2-hour gradings every two months and then suddenly face a long 5–6-hour grading for their significant Dan grade, we still held Dan gradings every six months. This meant students completed two smaller gradings before a larger, longer, and more intense grading twice a year.

Our all-school gradings followed this schedule:

- January, March, May, July, September, November

- Black Belt gradings were held every May and November

I have graduated over 250 Black Belts, but probably only 40 went on to achieve 2nd Dan. However, once we implemented the new grading system, the retention from 1st to 2nd Dan went through the roof. Students could no longer sit back, get bored, and drop out.

Don't get me wrong—the students were not being 'beasted' in every grading. But at the same time, they weren't coasting along for 22 months and then training hard for the last two months before their major Dan grading. Have you had students do that before?

CIT Programme

When students passed their Black Belt, they were automatically enrolled onto our Certified Instructor Training (CIT) programme. This was not optional—every student was enrolled. There was no discussion; they knew well in advance that earning their Black Belt meant becoming a trainee instructor.

I explained to my team, who then explained it to the students: *Your role as a Black Belt is to help other students develop, and the best way to do that is to teach them.*

At my discretion, we could enrol students onto the CIT programme from any grade after they had completed one year of training and committed to becoming a Black Belt. This meant they were either on the 'Black Belt Training' programme or our 'Masters & Leadership' programme.

This did *not* mean we had green belts standing at the front of the class teaching full lessons—no way. What it did mean was that we started to educate them on how to teach. We covered topics like:

- How to set up equipment

- Their positioning

- Their terminology

- Their body language

- Timing

- Keeping the mats clean and tidy

- Plus much more

We were always looking for soft skills—were they friendly and approachable? Did they have empathy? Their technical karate skills might not have been the best, but if they were a nice person and demonstrated the values of our Black Belt creed, that spoke volumes.

Linking this back to parents visiting our school for the first time, they wanted to see nice, respectful students their child could look up to. They didn't want to see cocky, arrogant students who thought they were above others just because they had a Black Belt. Your Black Belts should be genuinely good people with great character who truly believe in your programme.

Chapter 42

Black Belt Prep Cycle

Twice a year, we held our special Black Belt-only gradings. These were six months apart and took place every May and November. So, during a 12-month period, if a student wanted to stay on track, they would take part in six testings—four 'normal' gradings and two 'Black Belt-only' gradings.

The 'normal' gradings took place every two months and covered striped or full-colour belts. The 'Black Belt-only' gradings were for those attempting Black Belt or those who were already Black Belts.

The Black Belt prep cycle was a six-week cycle that took place six to seven weeks before one of the Black Belt gradings. This created such a buzz among students, and the biggest part of it was that it fostered 'esprit de corps'. With each cycle, we retained more and more students. I do not exaggerate—holding this Black Belt prep cycle was like flipping a switch on Black Belt retention.

If you are doing what I did for the first 15 years—letting students achieve Black Belt and then hoping they stick around for two years, during which time they could (if they wanted to) attend progress gradings—your students will leave in droves. They need to progress and see tangible rewards. The waiting period is too long, and they will be off pursuing other ventures.

How many times have you heard, 'They're just going to take a break,' only for them never to be seen again? It is your duty to keep hold of your Black Belts—they have invested in your school, and you have invested in them. The more Black Belts you retain, the more future instructors you have to develop.

The Black Belt Prep Cycle

The cycle consisted of two lessons per week for six weeks. To be eligible for grading, students could only miss a maximum of two lessons. Their attendance and effort during the cycle all contributed to their grading mark.

Rather than allowing students to be arrogant, cheeky, or disrespectful yet technically gifted for the four-hour grading, we aimed to build true character. Students were also judged on their team spirit and how they helped others, especially younger students. Higher grades mentored lower grades, helping to develop their leadership skills while enhancing their own knowledge.

When we planned the Black Belt prep cycle, we ensured that in addition to the 12 scheduled lessons, we had space for one or two bonus lessons. These were not included in the Black Belt prep schedule given to students, and they were only announced one week before they took place. These sessions often occurred at 7:15 am on a Saturday morning or on a Friday evening.

This was beneficial for two reasons:

1. It allowed students who had missed a lesson to make it up and still be eligible for grading.

2. It revealed who was truly committed and willing to attend at different or earlier times.

The Black Belt Prep Cycle Pack

When students first enrolled in our school, they are provided with a progress folder which amongst many things is to track their self-discipline achievements. They brought this folder to class so that instructors could see what they had been working on outside of our school. This folder remained with them throughout their trial enrolment programme and was only upgraded when they renewed onto one of the Black Belt training programmes.

During the Black Belt prep cycle, students were issued a special Black Belt Prep Pack.

The pack wasn't anything fancy—probably 8 to 12 pages long—but it included:

- The dates of the Black Belt prep lessons.

- Sections for students to reflect on how they had improved since being a White Belt.

- For 2nd dans, a section identifying who they were mentoring and explaining how they had developed since their 1st dan.

- A fitness tracker for the cycle.

- Tips on what to do before, during, and after their Black Belt grading.

The packs were handed in one week before the Black Belt grading, providing the panel with insights into what students had been doing to prepare.

You Don't Need to Lead Every Single Grading

By 2021, I had delivered well over 200 gradings—every single one led by me, apart from the two Black Belt gradings per year since 2008 (about 16 gradings in total) where I had a guest instructor sit on the panel with me. However, in 2021, I realised that my 1st and 2nd-degree team members were more than capable of handling the lower kyu grades (White, Yellow, Orange, and Green Belts).

After guiding them through this process, I then allowed them to grade Blue and Purple Belts. Eventually, I only attended the Black Belt gradings. This, in turn, placed more emphasis on those gradings.

Students would say things like, *'Sensei Dervish is doing the grading...'* or *'He's a 6th Dan...'* or *'I heard he failed students for making one wrong move in a kata!'*

I didn't mind that—it gave the Black Belt grading the edge I think it needs.

In summary, having a solid Black Belt Prep Cycle is another tool in your retention tool kit. Carried out properly it will improve your retention and contribute towards your school's growth.

Chapter 43

Your Ideal Black Belt Grading

We held under-belt gradings every two months, meaning we held six gradings a year. Significant Black Belt gradings were held twice a year, in May and November. Black Belts still took part in the under/lower belt gradings every two months but could only grade for significant Dan grades during May or November, i.e. 1st Dan, 2nd Dan, 3rd Dan, etc.

Ensuring gradings were held every two months was another incentive to keep ALL students grading regularly. Students need to see progression. Whatever got them to Black Belt will keep them at Black Belt. You cannot realistically expect a student who has been grading every two months (or every three to four months, depending on your current structure) since White Belt to suddenly earn a Black Belt and then not do a grading for two years.

As I get older, the more I realise we live in a society of instant gratification. Like me, you are likely wired differently. That is something martial arts has taught you—you need to work hard for things before you are rewarded. There's nothing wrong with that, and it's a mindset I'm trying to instil in my children and all my students.

Black Belt Progression

We wanted Black Belts to grade every two months, like the rest of the student body. We, therefore, decided there would be 12 gradings from 1st to 2nd Dan over a 24-month period. At each grading, they were awarded a tab. We wanted students to achieve nine tabs out of a possible 12 gradings.

If they needed nine tabs out of a possible 12, they could afford to miss three gradings and still be on track. (I felt this was very lenient.) If they missed four or more, then they had to wait an additional six months until the next Black Belt grading.

Another mistake I made was offering 'make-up gradings' for students who fell behind. This caused problems because they were learning a different syllabus compared to what they were grading on. I initially felt that offering these 'make-up gradings' was good for retention, but what really happened was students realised a 'make-up grading' would soon be available, which gave them more slack.

When students passed their Black Belt grading, we always provided them with a congratulations pack, which doubled up as a 'how to get to 2nd Degree Black Belt' roadmap. This pack contained:

- The Black Belt tab structure

- Their grading months

- When the next Black Belt prep cycle was likely to be

- Another goal-setting sheet

- A sheet for them to confirm their weekly teaching/leadership times

Each Black Belt had to help out at least once per week—90% did two lessons because they simply attended the lesson before or after their normal lesson. Their weekly teaching/leadership sheet was handed back in, and once we had all the sheets, we created a CIT timetable. This ensured that for every day of the week and for every TE lesson, we knew how many CITs to expect.

From brown belt onwards, we continually educated students on what being a Black Belt looked like. From reading this book, it should be clear just how much Black Belt played a part in EVERY single lesson—whether it was visualisation, benefits, goal-setting sheets, goal-setting season (held the month leading up to the significant Black Belt gradings), Black Belt Skills for Success & Attitude sheets, or personal development chats. If a student has been with you for one month, they need to know that you are a Black Belt school and that we expect students to train to Black Belt.

On the Black Belt Grading Day/Weekend

From 2008 to 2018, we held very long Black Belt gradings, scheduled for four to five hours. These were intense gradings. They were not the kind where hundreds of students were on the mats, coming up to the front in groups of ten, performing certain techniques for their Senseis for five to ten minutes, and then sitting down for 30 minutes. No way! I didn't have the active count for that anyway.

I often had non-Black Belt students enrol from other 'clubs' and say, "Why are your gradings only 1.5 hours long?" They would then go on to tell me they had been doing four-hour gradings at their previous clubs. I knew, however, that this style of grading for lower belts was just a round-robin approach—white belts perform a technique, then sit down; yellow belts perform a technique, then sit down; orange belts do the same, and so on. In reality, students were only active for about 10–15% of the grading.

My Black Belt gradings were very intense because I wanted my students to feel that they had truly earned their belt. Looking back, it was like I was putting them through SAS training. I was young then, and I wanted them all to be machines. I pushed them through an intense kihon (basics) section, followed by a rigorous sparring section. Everything back then was about fitness and not being a quitter—I wanted them to have my mindset.

From 2019, I adopted a longer, weekend-style grading. This was another process I dragged my feet on. I was always stuck in 'analysis paralysis' when learning about new approaches. I was guilty of buying books on sales, marketing, best business practices, and coaching, reading them, creating a list of things I should implement, and then only doing one or two because I was contemplating the rest.

I used to say things like, "What will my students think? What will the parents think? It's new, and I don't know if it will work," etc. It then dawned on me that one of my own team training sayings— "That's the way it's always been done"—was not something I should be applying to Black Belt gradings or my own thought process.

Rest assured, if you decide to work with me to grow your school, I will hold you accountable because I want you to grow a successful business.

To give you some context, we had about eight to ten team sayings that we repeated in most team meetings and constantly reminded each other of during the day when situations arose. (See Bonus Section at the back of this book for all the sayings.) We called these our 'team sayings.' Another important one was: "Never assume."

If we wanted to become a professional Black Belt school, we needed to improve our Black Belt gradings. The gradings we had been doing were just 'more of the same.' Students still had to complete all syllabus sections, but the only difference compared to under-belts was that it lasted longer and was more intense. While this was good—because they really had to earn their Black Belt—I wanted to professionalise it further. I wanted the Black Belt grading to stand out.

Having a longer Black Belt grading, combined with the Black Belt preparation cycle and holding the under-belt gradings on the same day, MASSIVELY enhanced the professionalism of our school.

Think of it this way—under-Black Belts only see Black Belts in passing when entering or leaving your school, or they might be helped by them in class (hopefully, if you have a CIT programme). However, they rarely see them 'in action.' They should witness their laser-sharp focus, discipline, and determination. Younger students might be inspired by Black Belts when they teach them, but they will be even more inspired when they see them in a grading environment—when they should be at their best.

How the Black Belt Grading Weekend Would Look

Friday Evening

- 6:00 - 9:00 PM Black Belt Grading Pt 1

Saturday

- 7:00 - 8:30 AM Black Belt Grading Pt 2

  o 15-minute break

- 8:45 - 10:00 AM *(Testing their leadership skills in the beginner grading)*

  o 15-minute break

- 10:15 - 11:45 AM *(Testing their leadership skills in the intermediate grading and joining in certain sections)*

  o 30-minute lunch break

- 12.15-2.15pm Black Belt Grading Pt 3

  o 15-minute break

- 2.30-3.30pm Black Belt Grading Pt 4

- All-school graduation at 4:00 PM

Grading for lower-grade (under Black Belt) students is marked with an asterisk ()*

Content Covered

Friday Evening

6-9pm Black Belt Grading Pt 1

- Kihon, which consists of basics, basic kicks, kicking combinations, stances, hokei techniques, sparring, and kata.

- This is the 3Ks part of the grading: Kihon, Kata, Kumite.

Saturday

7-8.30am Black Belt Grading Pt 2

- Padwork

  o 15-minute break

8:45 - 10:00 AM *(Testing their leadership skills in the beginner grading)*

- A mixture of students shadowing and assisting others, calling commands, etc.

  o 15-minute break

10:15 - 11:45 AM *(Testing their leadership skills in the intermediate grading and joining in certain sections)*

- They participate in the self-defence portion of the grading.

  o 30-minute break

12:15 - 2:15 PM

- Kata, bunkai, weapons, plus anything else we may have run out of time to cover.

  o 15-minute break

2:30 - 3:30 PM

- More sparring and conditioning.

All-school graduation at 4:00 PM

Adapting the Format

The structure above can be adjusted depending on your school and the number of active students. You could spread it over a Saturday and Sunday or extend the times, but whatever you do, it must feel different from your normal under-belt gradings.

There should be a buzz in the 6-7 weeks leading up to Black Belt gradings. This has several benefits:

1. It gets the grading students into the right mindset.

2. It encourages lower-grade students to start thinking about Black Belt.

I know I keep emphasising this, but your parents and students need to be consistently thinking about and visualising Black Belt. Instructors should be making regular announcements, sending emails, and talking with EVERY parent. Paper reminders should be handed out in class.

Your goal is 100% of students grading and ensuring their parent or guardian attends the graduation to celebrate their success.

Building a Strong Black Belt Culture

Having a structured Black Belt prep cycle, grading students every two months, and incorporating a weekend-style grading significantly improves retention. If you've read books on teamwork, you may be familiar with the phrase *esprit de corps*—this preparation cycle fosters and strengthens that spirit.

During the cycle, students work as a unit. Although martial arts is an individual discipline, this process brings them together as a team. Nobody wants to let their teammates down.

Making the Black Belt Award Special

When awarding Black Belts, don't just hand out an A4 certificate printed on your home computer (like I used to back in the day). Instead, we used professionally designed A3 certificates, printed on thick 300gsm paper and presented in a high-quality frame. These cost around £12 each instead of the £2 cheap ones, but they made a real difference.

The entire grading panel of Senseis was present for photos, making the occasion stand out from all previous gradings.

Don't scrimp on your students. If they've been training with you for four or more years, think about how much they have contributed to your school. Investing in quality certificates and frames is a small price to pay for their dedication. Some of these students will become your next full-time instructors, so take care of them.

Chapter 44

Instructor Training – Build From Within

In my experience, I have always found that the best team members are homegrown.

"Don't hire externally" would be a bit of advice I would give based on being an employer. I made the mistake of trying to hire from outside our school. The principle sounded good—anybody who was a brown belt or above could apply for the position, we would teach them our ways, and if it worked out well, we would recruit more and more instructors, allowing us to scale.

At this stage, I was still a bit hazy on the direction I wanted to take the business. All I was concerned about was the growth of the bottom line. I could have concentrated on making our single school 125% efficient, started to build out satellites, or opened franchises. I was lucky to have options.

I would recommend anybody reading this to make their single location/school as profitable as possible before even considering opening satellite venues or franchising. This comes down to the economy of scale. It is much easier to gain more members, hold more classes at a single school than to establish a new location where your overheads can double overnight, but the revenue remains the same. Don't always fall for the "bigger is better" mantra. The mantra you need to follow is: "Turnover is vanity—profit is sanity."

I know many "sports club" businesses that, because their classes had 15+ people in them (when they were used to only 6-8), thought they needed to get another venue. What a terrible mistake they made. They didn't consider things like staffing, systems, standardisation, and most importantly, their bottom line. Build one school and make it as profitable as possible.

You NEED to build your instructors from within, and they also need to have a clear mission that they can buy into and contribute towards.

Once students have committed to training to Black Belt, you should be looking at them and cherry-picking who you think would be a good fit for your instructor team. This is not based on their technical ability, competition record, or physical fitness. The skills I used to look for in team members were:

- Did they have big egos? (This was a negative.)

- Could they converse with people?

- Were they approachable?

- Were they positive and polite?

- Would they be a good follower? (That's not a bad thing.) Did they understand the hierarchy of the school?

- Ultimately, were they a nice person who would care for the students?

I wanted team members that parents and students would feel comfortable talking to. You don't want students saying, "I don't want to come on Sundays because it's Sensei [Name] teaching." They might not like a particular instructor because of how they speak to the class or their child. From a parent's point of view, the instructor's technical skills won't even come into question—it's all about how they make their child feel.

With a team of 10 paid members at one point, with a payroll of over £12-£14k per month, I know most of the problems that can arise. 95% of the time, it was all good, but 5% of the time, it was a headache. As your team grows, so does your knowledge of leadership and management.

How Do You Build the Team?

Don't wait until they are Black Belt. As soon as they have committed to a Black Belt training programme, you want to start introducing tiny leadership elements to them. They are not teaching the class, but they can start to help it run. They can assist the main instructor. Some examples include:

- Greeting people as they enter

- Collecting attendance cards at the beginning of a lesson

- Setting up cones, hurdles, or other equipment for the warm-up

- Holding pads for younger students

- Helping younger students on a one-to-one basis

- Awarding character tabs

- Awarding a certificate at the end

- Tidying the school at the end of the day

You are just getting them used to being in a different role than a student who follows instructions. You are bringing them from standing and facing the instructor and mirrors (if your school has mirrors) to standing at the front, facing the lowest grades. It's a different perspective for them.

As I mentioned earlier—don't wait until they are Black Belt to start their instructor training. I used to start instructor training from green belt, which was their third full-colour belt, meaning they had been at our school for 12 months. Let me repeat here—they were not leading the class. However, if I thought they had excellent interpersonal skills and were naturally a nice, friendly person, I would start at orange belt (meaning they had been at our school for eight months).

The longer you have to mould them, the better an instructor they will be. The more they shadow you, the more they will be like you. My first two full-time instructors were like clones of me—their energy, timing, vocabulary, efficiency, and pace. You don't want there to be too much contrast between your instructors. If this happens, you end up back at, "I don't like coming on Mondays because Sensei X teaches then." Regardless of who is teaching, the same content should be covered in the same format as the lead instructor.

When students entered their third year with us and were earning their first brown belt (3rd Kyu), this was when we formalised the training for them. They had a CIT booklet where they needed to track and log their teaching experience. Plus, each grading cycle (approximately 8-9 weeks), they had to work on two main things: warm-ups, kicking sections, kata, pad work, character tabs, etc.

The more we developed them as brown belts and built on their leadership and confidence, the better they would be when they earned their Black Belt. Our highest-level programme was called "Masters and Leadership"—but how could they be classed as a leader if they were not building on their leadership skills every week, month, and year? If you are shaping and moulding your CITs from green belt, just imagine how good an instructor they will be when they earn their Black Belt.

Teaching Experience

My first ever teaching experience was horrendous. It was in 1999, and I was a 2nd or 1st Kyu. I had to teach 30+ students in a classroom where the desks and chairs had been pushed to the sides. It was an absolute car crash. I was 17 years old and had never even done a warm-up before, never mind delivered an entire class.

The class consisted of white belts all the way up to Black, all mixed grades (something you should not do when designing your school). I had no teaching experience before this, other than standing in front of white belts doing their kicking combinations super slowly so they could follow. Our Sensei used to rotate brown belts to stand in front of the white belts.

Now, when I opened my own school, I was very efficient at teaching a mixed class of different grades, ages, and abilities. I was teaching six days a week and delivering 13 lessons each week (two lessons Monday-Thursday, one lesson on Friday, and four lessons on Saturday).

You need to constantly build your team from within. They know your systems and what should happen and when. When you bring somebody in from outside, they have to learn all of this. I'm not saying that's impossible—not at all—but it is much harder compared to somebody who has been picking it up for 2-3-4-5 years. You have had a lot of time to tweak their teaching so that it is exactly how you want it.

Your students will subconsciously pick up the format of your lessons. They will know how long a warm-up should last, how the first bow should go, when to do class announcements, etc. They will know your systems and won't say things like, "Well, at my other club, we used to do it this way."

Constantly add to your pool of CITs, knowing that some will inevitably drop off. I always used to use the "think of Manchester United" example. Unfortunately, they are nowhere near the dominant team they used to be under Sir Alex Ferguson, but most people will remember that Manchester United were very dominant during the 1990s.

Before we carry on, I'm not a football fan—I just admire great coaches like Sir Alex Ferguson and Phil Jackson. When Manchester United or the Chicago Bulls were dominating everything, I don't think they looked at their bench and said, "I can't play him because he's rubbish." Yes, the person on the bench may have been slightly different from the players who started the game, but the skill set and talent level were not massively different. At that elite level, there are often only minor differences.

Your role, as someone trying to build a business, is to have a strong bench so that not every single class, seminar, grading, pre-grading class, primary school class, enrolment conference, or phone call needs to be handled by you. That was me back in 2004–2014. Don't fall for the "I need to do everything because I'm the best at it" mentality.

I once read that if somebody can do something 70% as well as you, then you should let them do it every time. If you are the best at it, then train somebody else to do it just as well as you can. As you progress, you should be looking to delegate the lower-value jobs— the tasks that don't move the dial much—while you concentrate on the higher-value tasks, i.e. the tasks that cause the dial to move the most: marketing and sales (enrolments and renewals) and team training.

As you grow, the last elements you should step away from—should you choose to do so—are marketing, enrolment conferences, and renewal conferences.

How do you know if an instructor is good?

An instructor may be technically gifted, but in addition to the qualities mentioned above, I would also be looking at:

- Retention: Have our retention figures improved since they started?

- Creating value: Do they have the correct balance between physical and developmental aspects?

- Are there lots of red jackets in their lessons?

- Are they continually inspiring students to be better in their lives?

- Do they write sincere, awesome letters rather than just "well done"?

- Do they go above and beyond?

- Are their students engaged in the self-discipline programme?

- Do their lessons start and finish on time?

Your Mission...

This is something you need to create and explain to your team. If it's a clear mission, it won't need much explanation.

For example, it could be: *To positively impact as many students in our town as possible through teaching our unique character development programme.*

Be aware of having a financial goal as a mission, e.g. *to take over £20k in tuition each month and to have a revenue of over £250k per year.* Financial goals are good, but your mission needs to be more deep-rooted and meaningful. Your mission is something that should continually pull your school forward.

In summary, start to build your team now. The more time you spend with them the better it will be for your school and students.

Chapter 45

Don't Make These Mistakes With Your Team

How Did I Start?

When I first started my 'club' back in 2004, it was a little 'side hustle'. I had no intention of turning it into a full-time job or making a good living from it. I was in my second year of university, still living at home, and working part-time at a supermarket on weekends.

I was speaking to one of my karateka friends, who was training for his 3rd dan at the time. I was lamenting about working in a supermarket and feeling like I could do more. In passing, he said, *"Why don't you start a little club? You enjoy karate, and I think you'd be good at it."*

I didn't give it much thought at first, but a few days later, I found myself thinking it wasn't a bad idea. I was selling it to myself—*I could teach karate, earn a few extra pounds… it'll be money for old rope.*

That, really, is how Kaizen-Do Karate started.

I went looking for venues well outside my town (another stupid mistake). I found a venue in the function room of a low-end snooker hall (mistake), put up a few homemade A4 posters in cafés (better than nothing, but still a mistake), and that was it.

Looking back now, I made so many mistakes in the first 8–10 years of running my 'club'. However, the best thing I did was take action. I didn't fall into *analysis paralysis*—something I want you to avoid.

Don't overthink everything that could go wrong. Just focus on one or two things a day that you need to do.

If you're reading this and don't have a member base or a venue yet, you need to start advertising, then find a venue. If you already have a member base and are operating, my experience tells me that you need to work on your marketing and creating value for your programme. Open your mind to the possibility that your school is nowhere near as successful as it could be. It may only be grossing 5-10% of what is actually possible.

The Control Freak Years

For the first 7–8 years, I taught every single lesson, seminar, private lesson, pre-grading lesson, grading, and primary school class—I did EVERYTHING. I was a control freak. This was my baby, and if I wanted something done properly, I had to do it myself. I didn't want to pass any job—no matter how unimportant—onto anybody else.

The biggest thing holding me back was not having adults coming through who could one day become instructors I could rely on. I think the first time I handed a class over to another instructor was around 2012. Even then, I stayed on the mats to micromanage.

I didn't have the best CIT programme back then, and as a result, the lessons were just karate lessons. The CIT programme was basically a Japanese-English test of common techniques, how to deliver a warm-up, and that was it. As a result, there was a huge difference between when I taught and when other instructors taught.

I'm not saying they were bad—far from it. They were my students from white belt, so they were homegrown. However, what was noticeable was my emphasis on personal development, keeping the lesson pace moving, preventing students from interrupting every three seconds, not giving long, detailed explanations of each technique, and challenging students appropriately to their grade, plus much more.

Again, this was 100% my fault. I didn't build *bench strength*, and my instructor programme wasn't comprehensive enough. You need to start shaping and moulding your instructors from Year 2 onwards. Eventually, we started instructor training for green belts and above—after 12 months of training at our school. They weren't teaching lessons; they were assisting—setting up cones, running warm-ups, awarding character tabs, and shadowing white belts.

The Reality of Owning a Job, Not a Business

At one point, I was working 8am–8pm Monday to Friday and 8am–4pm on Saturdays. I then did admin-based tasks on Saturday night or Sunday.

I didn't mind this because I was building my business. The more I worked, the more I earned. I was paying for it in sweat equity, and I didn't have any debt—which wasn't a bad thing. However, in hindsight, I didn't own a *business* at all—I owned a *job*.

Can you relate to this?

If I was sick, so what? I still had to teach class and do everything else that needed doing. It was the classic *E-Myth* story by Michael E. Gerber.

I didn't want to pay people or cover their National Insurance contributions, pension contributions, sick pay, holiday pay, and everything else that came with it. It sounded like a headache, and I wanted to keep as much money as I could. Back then, I had a *scarcity mindset* rather than an *abundance mindset*.

I was young and liked earning what I thought was good money at the time. By around 28 years old, I was making anywhere from £1000–£1,400 per week—around £7k per month—from my *side hustle*. I still hadn't gone full-time and was still working as a lecturer.

The problem was, I had fallen into the *trading time for money* trap.

There's nothing wrong with trading time for money, but to make more money, you need to work more hours or raise your rates. If you want to grow your school into a profitable business, you need team members you can delegate to. There's a limit to how profitable your school can be if you're both head chef and chief dishwasher.

Mistakes I Made with Great Team Members (That I Ended Up Losing)

- Expecting them to work as hard and as long as me. I had some great instructors with a strong work ethic, but I expected too much.

- Wanting them to reply to emails within one minute of me sending them—regardless of the time or day.

- Expecting them to work six days a week without complaints.

- Not being as understanding as I could have been.

Hindsight is a wonderful thing. If I could do it over, I would set their working week to just five days. Or, if they preferred 8am–8pm shifts, then obviously, just four days a week.

I assumed they were the same as me and motivated by money. If *you* are motivated by money, let me tell you—not everyone is. Not everyone wants to be wealthy or have the finer things in life. Some people are happy as long as they have enough to meet their needs. I know plenty of family members like that—and that's fine.

I'm part of mastermind and mentor groups, where I'm surrounded by fellow entrepreneurs who all want to build something and make a good living. But those people are not the majority.

Things I Would Try to Accommodate If Starting Again:

- Let them have their birthdays off.

- Allow them to swap their shifts.

- Work 4–5 days per week.

During my first couple of years as an employer, I often let people coast along even when I knew they were not contributing as much as they could. A good management mantra is *hire slowly and fire quickly*. As the years progressed, I became less tolerant of underperformance. At the end of the day, keeping someone on when they're not meeting expectations does no one any favours—you're continuing to pay someone for substandard performance, they're not helping to grow your school, and you're preventing them from finding a role they might genuinely enjoy. Get rid of them and move on.

Another great reason to introduce your CIT programme is that it acts as a long-term job interview over two, three, four, or even five years. You get to see their attendance, punctuality, and willingness to take on feedback.

The thing is, I wanted to grow a highly profitable martial arts school—I didn't just want to run a small club with two classes a week where everyone trains together. I wanted to be known as the best, not for competition records but for producing students who were great individuals—students who embodied respect, focus, discipline, and determination. I wanted to inspire them to have goals and to believe they could achieve whatever they set their minds to.

I could not have grown the school to over £30k per month by being an easy-going leader. However, as a result of my high expectations, I often burned my Senseis out. I could only keep them for two to three years before they moved on.

In summary, don't overwork your team. If you look after them, they will, in turn, look after your students—which ultimately means looking after your business.

Part 7
SUMMARY

Dervish Dervish

Summary

You got there – well done!

Depending on how you have been reading this book—whether one chapter a day, a week, or all in one sitting because you've had your eyes opened to how your school could run—just remember that there are hundreds of factors that contribute to your school's success.

I haven't even covered everything I know about running a school in this book, but hopefully, it has proven that I do know how to build a successful, thriving, and profitable school—and that my mentees greatly benefit from working with me.

Of course, I can help you improve, and I have a proven formula for success. You have plenty to get stuck into, and the important thing is that I could have gone into much more detail in every single chapter. There are even some elements I haven't mentioned (I might leave those for the second book).

If you are truly serious about improving your school's standards, building a successful business, and earning a professional salary for your work, then contact me. We can discuss your goals and see if we are a good fit for each other. Just check out the *What Should You Do Now* chapter.

What You Should Do Now?

Hopefully, this book has opened your mind to the endless opportunities available to build your school and create the lifestyle you deserve. You owe it to the hundreds—if not thousands—of students you have yet to meet.

Contact me NOW to book your **FREE** consultation.

The options you have moving forward are quite simple:

a) Put the book on your shelf and lie to yourself, saying you will implement some of the ideas.

b) Go it alone, struggle, and make small steps forward.

c) Contact me so I can help grow your school to outstanding levels and exponetially grow your profits.

I can guarantee you will go further with the correct guidance—just as you have done in your own martial art.

Why Invest In A Mentor?

They share their decades of experience and mistakes, ultimately fast-tracking your journey to success—that is exactly what I do for my mentees.

Whatever you decide to do, you must keep learning. As a martial artist, you probably already have that *Kaizen* mindset—just transfer that quest for knowledge and self-improvement into building your school. If you have a thirst for knowledge and wisdom and apply what you learn, you will be successful.

It would be great to speak with you, so get in touch for a FREE consultation. You can provide me with a picture of your school and share what you're looking to achieve, and we can work on bringing that vision to life.

If you decide you want to take your school, business, and life to the next level, don't hesitate—get in touch NOW! I can help accelerate your growth, teach you the finer principles, and share some great concepts not covered in this book.

Thank you very much for reading the book—I hope you enjoyed it. I would greatly appreciate it if you could leave me a 5-star review.

Wishing you, your family, and your students all the best.

Dervish Dervish

Part 8
BONUS SECTION

Included in this section are a few items that may help you better understand some of the topics covered in the main part of this book.

The following are included:

- **BONUS SECTION 1:** Don't make these mistakes in your school

- **BONUS SECTION 2:** Single school or multi-location?

- **BONUS SECTION 3:** Team sayings

- **BONUS SECTION 4:** Templates for some certificates and signs

- **BONUS SECTION 5:** Our programme and levels

BONUS SECTION 1
Don't Make These
Mistakes In Your School

1. Charging anywhere near what everybody else around you is charging.

2. Not having a clear sales/enrolment process.

3. Not having a clear and detailed marketing plan.

4. Not having a renewal process.

5. Not doing enough—action = results.

6. Thinking that because you're a 2nd, 3rd, or 4th Dan, anybody is bothered.

7. Going on about your lineage and how pure it is.

8. Pulling back on marketing because you're getting too many new members.

9. Not marketing consistently.

10. Not having scripts for dealing with initial enquiries.

11. Not tracking stats.

12. Having a huge school with loads of fitness equipment.

13. Being stuck in analysis paralysis.

14. Letting instructors give discounts on tuition.

15. Thinking you know it all as soon as your gross income goes up—keep learning.

16. Not marketing intensively for the first 10–12 years.

17. Just teaching physical skills, i.e. 'kicks and punches'.

18. Not making changes quickly enough when stats weren't on track.

19. Not charging what my programme was worth.

20. Not implementing a rotating curriculum.

21. Not introducing striped belts.

22. Not testing Black Belts regularly.

23. Not addressing the Black Belt dropout that used to happen upon achieving 1st Degree.

24. Not having a separate CIT/Sensei training programme for students to complete.

25. Getting students to do contact sparring straight away.

26. Not having a CIT programme.

27. Thinking you have to teach every single class, seminar, progress check, grading, etc.

28. Not doing enough staff training.

29. Not scheduling regular staff training.

30. Not having a clearly defined enrolment process.

31. Worrying about what other 'clubs' and instructors might think or say.

32. Using silly barcode systems instead of a good old-fashioned attendance card.

33. Not tracking dropouts closely.

34. Not trying to bring ex-members back into the fold.

35. Learning new things but then sitting on them for months or years.

36. Feeling overwhelmed and not taking action.

37. Having all students in the same programme and not securing a commitment to Black Belt training.

38. Running silly holiday programmes just to bring in extra money because that's what other sports activities do.

39. My biggest mistake, not investing in a mentor sooner.

That's just a quick list of 39 mistakes I made during the first 12 years of running my school. I urge you to learn from my mistakes and invest in a mentor if you want to grow a profitable, sustainable business.

Single Location or Multi School?

You should stick to a single location at first to maximise your gross income in relation to your fixed expenses. I know several businesses that used to say, *"Our classes are getting too full—we need to open a new location."* As soon as they took that dreaded step, their expenses (mostly rent) doubled overnight.

That meant that, to maintain the same profit percentage compared to gross income as when their classes were "too full," they needed to double their membership base. While doubling your membership base isn't impossible, it's not an easy task—especially if you already have an active count of 100+ members.

I can think of four businesses that did this, only to shut down their additional locations within six months. They didn't fully consider the logistics. For example, if an instructor calls in sick at a single venue, another team member or CIT can cover. However, if you have multiple locations, who covers when there's an issue at one site? This leads to a disconnect in quality and service.

If I were starting over, I wouldn't have any aspirations to build a chain of schools. Instead, I would focus on creating the most efficient and profitable single school, requiring zero (or as close to zero) effort from me.

Don't fall into the trap of thinking that just because you have two or three locations, you are a big business owner running a super-profitable company. I would much rather have one school generating £25,000 per month than three locations bringing in £7,000–£8,000 per month each.

Don't create unnecessary headaches for yourself—focus on making your single school as efficient as possible. To do this, you need to:

- Consistently market your school.

- Analyse your timetable regularly.

- Identify which classes are too busy or too quiet and tweak them accordingly.

- Learn from professionals

Remember, your school is likely empty (without students) for about 20 hours a day. Why double your overheads by securing another lease when your existing location still has so much room for growth?

Make your operation slick, efficient, and highly profitable—not big, cumbersome, costly, and barely making a profit.

BONUS SECTION 3
Team Sayings

The following is a small sample of the team sayings that evolved as we built our team. Team members learned most of these during their orientation training. Behind each saying, there was always at least one example of how it came about. The main purpose of these sayings was to help both team members and our company improve.

If a team member asked a question, I or another team member could often answer it with one of the sayings. For example:

"I'm unsure if we should invite a student to Black Belt training—they've been here four months."

The answer was simple: *"Students on Basic quit—commit or quit."*

The following team sayings are in no particular order:

Be Nice

Treat members and fellow team members as you wish to be treated.

Students on Basic Quit – Commit or Quit!

If students do not enrol onto M&L (or BBT), they quit.

Don't Let Students Die on the Vine

Students value and appreciate our programmes very early in their journey—typically within the first six weeks. This is when we should renew them.

GSD – Get Stuff Done

This phrase often came up with part-timers who would ask, *"Sensei, what should I do?"* No sooner had they pronounced the *'d'* in *'do'* than a more experienced team member would shout, *"GSD!"*

...or GLSD – Get Loads of Stuff Done

We all have tasks we are accountable for. Rather than procrastinate—get working!

Respect the Systems

Systems have been designed to ensure consistency—don't ignore them. Follow them to achieve the best outcomes.

Never Assume (Always Clarify)

This is a common rule in most businesses. For us, it was particularly relevant when making confirmation calls. Just because someone said they were coming—and even confirmed yesterday—does not mean they are coming today. A team member should *never assume*, but always clarify. Unless you know the definitive answer, you must clarify.

If We See It, They See It

If we notice a piece of rubbish on the floor, our students will also see it.

Touch It, Finish It

Don't jump from task to task, and don't throw the task to another team member. Multi-tasking is not as efficient as completing one task at a time.

Time to Lean Means Time to Clean

This comes from Ray Kroc (the man who took McDonald's global). It means there is always something to do. If you feel there's nothing to do—clean!

Don't Get Stuck in Analysis Paralysis

Perfectionism is paralysis. Your chief goal should be maximum profit. *Good enough (GE) is good enough.* Find out where the GE spot is—what is truly important to *them*, not what *we* think is important.

For example, the GE spot for answering the phone should be by the third ring at the latest. If we don't answer, we risk invisible losses—because the caller will simply ring a competitor.

1440

When someone says, *"I haven't had time,"* they're usually wrong—they just haven't used their time efficiently. We all have 1,440 minutes in a day. Use them wisely.

Hot Potato (a.k.a. Don't Manage Up)

When team members encountered an obstacle, they were expected to find a solution—not simply say, *"Sensei, I can't do this, will you do it?"*

New starters were given some allowances, but experienced team members were expected to find their own solutions.

If You're on Time, You're Late

If you are expected to start work at 8am on a Saturday, you should be ready to start at 8am—not walking through the door at 8am while messing with your phone.

If you let punctuality slip, other standards will slip too. Everything matters.

"That's the Way It's Always Been Done"

This phrase used to make me cringe. If there was no justifiable reason why a task was done a certain way, then we could change it.

If It's Everybody's Job, It's Nobody's Job

We assigned a clear person to each task/system. If something broke down, we knew who to go to. If *everyone* was responsible for a task, that ultimately meant *nobody* was in charge.

Eyes Up

Whenever a team member was behind the front desk, they needed to maintain an "eyes up" approach. We didn't want prospects or existing students walking in without being greeted with a friendly smile.

As you grow your school and your team, you will create your own team sayings. They will help build a stronger unit and a better understanding of your school's goals.

BONUS SECTION 4
Templates of some certificates and signs

As you have probably gathered, we ran a very systemised school, and as a result, we had many templates to ensure consistency throughout the team. Included here is just a small sample of the templates we used.

Class Certificates

The following are just some of the A5 certificates we awarded during classes. These certificates were awarded at the end of the class and students were asked to come to the front of the class so the other students could give them a round of applause.

Best Beginner

This certificate has a blue border.

Excellent Potential

This certificate has a purple border.

Black Belt Respect

Kaizen-Do Karate
★ EXCELLENT POTENTIAL ★

.... has shown
excellent effort in this class on ....

You are learning important LIFESKILLS
which will ultimately help you
become a better person.

Continue to train hard, learn all of our
LIFESKILLS and progress through our
levels, Black Belt and beyond.

LIFESKILL you have shown ....

'A Black Belt is a White belt that never quit'

Yours in Karate

Master Dervish, 6th Degree Black Belt.
BSc. (Hons). Sport & Exercise Science. PGCE.
Founder, Chief Instructor & Managing Director.
Kaizen-Do Karate; Martial Arts School.

THE
FAMILY MARTIAL ARTS ACADEMY

Building Character through Our Programmes
Goals + Commitment = Success

KaizenDoKarate.com

Star of the Class

This certificate has a red border.

Black Belt Determination

Kaizen-Do Karate
⭐ STAR OF THE CLASS ⭐

.... **has shown**
excellent effort in this class on ....

You are learning important LIFESKILLS
which will ultimately help you
become a better person.

Continue to train hard, learn all of our
LIFESKILLS and progress through our
levels, Black Belt and beyond.

LIFESKILL you have shown ....

'A Black Belt is a White belt that never quit'

Yours in Karate

Master Dervish, **6th Degree Black Belt.**
BSc. (Hons). Sport & Exercise Science. PGCE.
Founder, Chief Instructor & Managing Director.
Kaizen-Do Karate; Martial Arts School.

THE
FAMILY MARTIAL ARTS ACADEMY

Building Character through Our Programmes
Goals + Commitment = Success

KaizenDoKarate.com

Grading Certificates

The following are some of the A4 full-colour grading certificates we awarded at graduations:

Yellow Belt Certificate

This A4 certificate has a yellow border to match their new belt colour

Orange Belt Certificate

This A4 certificate has an orange border to match their new belt colour

Self-Discipline Sheets

We had many self-discipline sheets, all of which contributed to the value of our programme. Here is the Job List sheet we used to give to students to help them earn a character tab:

Self-Discipline Sheet – Job List

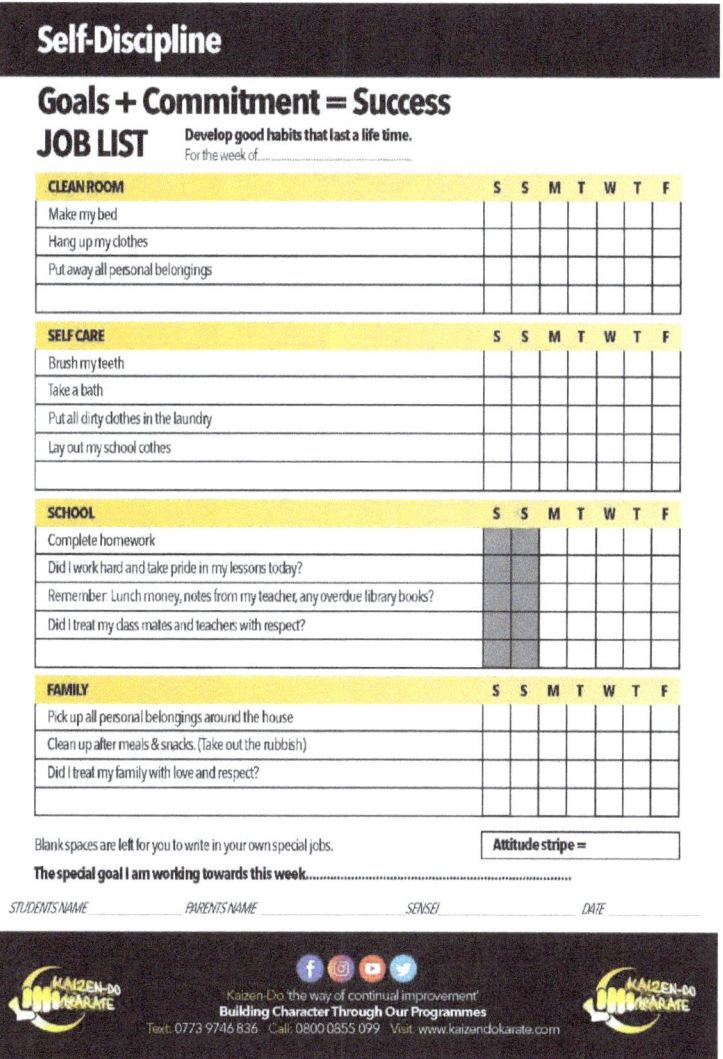

Self-Discipline Medals

Self-Discipline medals were awarded to students for completing a set number of self-discipline sheets for their level. Medals were presented at graduations.

Self-Discipline Medals –

Self-Discipline Awards

Self-discipline trophies were awarded to students for completing all self-discipline sheets for their level. The trophies were presented at graduations, serving as another excellent retention tool.

Awesome Job Letter

These were handwritten at the end of each day and awarded to two or three students who had not only tried really hard but, more importantly, demonstrated the behaviours we wanted to encourage. A team member would then post them that same day.

Awesome Job:

Black Belt Creed

The Black Belt Creed is another key element in your *We Are a Black Belt School* ethos. At the end of every lesson, we would conclude by reciting the Black Belt Creed.

Below is one of the signs we had displayed around our school. A printed version was also given to students during their trial orientation. Additionally, students had the opportunity to earn a character tab for confidently remembering and reciting the creed.

Black Belt Creed

BLACK BELT CREED

Karate For Concentration

As a dedicated student of the Martial Arts,
I live my life by the principles of Black Belt:

Modesty   **Courtesy**

Integrity   **Perseverance**

Self Control   **Indomitable Spirit**

Building Character Through Our Programmes
www.kaizendokarate.com

Kaizen-Do 'the way of continual improvement'

BONUS SECTION 5
Our programme and levels

This is a very basic overview of how our curriculum was structured.

Each block covered a four-month period. During that time, students progressed from one full-colour belt to the next. However, they also graded for a striped belt midway through the block, approximately every two months.

Year 1			
Belts	White going for Yellow	Yellow going for Orange	Orange going for Green
Trial enrolment + students committed to a Black Belt Training programme	Block 1	Block 2	Block 3
Year 2			
	Green-Blue	Blue-Purple	Purple-Purple 2 stripe
Only students committed to a Black Belt training programme	Block 1	Block 2	Block 3
Year 3			
	Purple 2 stripe -Brown 3rd Kyu	Brown 3rd Kyu - 3rd Kyu	Brown 3rd Kyu tab - 2nd Kyu
Only students committed to a Black Belt training programme	Block 1	Block 2	Block 3
Year 4			
	Brown 2nd Kyu – 2nd Kyu tab	Brown 2nd Kyu tab – 1st kyu	Brown 1st Kyu – 1 black stripe
Only students committed to a Black Belt training programme	Block 1	Block 2	Block 3
Year 5			
Only students committed to a Black Belt training programme	1 black stripe – 2 black stripes	Black Belt 1st Degree	

Final Reminder

If you are truly serious about improving your school and making a significant change in your life, then get in touch. I can help you enhance your operations, standards, and revenue, ultimately improving your lifestyle.

I've been in your position and achieved great success. I only choose to work with dedicated individuals who are willing to put in the effort. If that sounds like you, email me at:

hello@DervishMentoring.com

All the best.

Who is Sensei Dervish

Dervish Dervish is a successful mentor with over two decades of experience in business, property investment, and martial arts. Endorsed by Sensei David Turton, Europe's highest-graded self-defence instructor, Dervish—a 6th Degree Master Black Belt—has combined the principles of martial arts, such as discipline, resilience, and focus, with his passion for helping others achieve great success in business and personal growth.

From opening his first school in January 2004, he built a high-earning, highly profitable, self-sustaining martial arts school that grossed more in a month than the competition did in one to two years. He then turned his attention to property investment. In a very short period, he built a substantial portfolio that generates consistent passive income. By the age of 33, he had established a thriving martial arts school, paid off his mortgage, created a cash-flowing property portfolio, and achieved a lifestyle many strive for—all by applying his unique mindset and business strategies.

Through his unique mentoring approach, he empowers entrepreneurs to build wealth, create profitable, systemised businesses, and develop an unbreakable mindset that leads to long-term success and work-life balance.

Today, through his 1:1 mentoring, he equips mentees with a roadmap to build their ideal lives, combining actionable business systems, financial strategies, and mindset work.

Dervish's mentees are mostly martial arts school owners and property investors, all united by a common desire to reach new heights in their business and personal lives. He builds strong partnerships with his mentees, ensuring they feel supported, empowered, and challenged to reach their full potential. His hands-on approach and genuine dedication to client growth have helped countless individuals overcome self-doubt, develop resilience, and achieve remarkable results.

Dervish combines the best of personal development with business acumen. His mentorship goes beyond traditional coaching, offering mentees the tools, strategies, and mindset shifts needed to create a life of both prosperity and balance. He helps his mentees unlock their true potential and build their ideal life.

Work with him if you're ready to take your business to the next level.

Get in Touch

Thank you for purchasing your copy of *How to Build a Highly Profitable Martial Arts School.*

I have packed a lot of information into this book, and I hope you find it very useful.

I want you to grow a highly successful school and teach your art to thousands of students. Check out the following resources to help you on your business journey:

YouTube: Dervish_Dervish

If you would like more specific and tailored advice on how to grow your school, build a successful business, and increase your profits, feel free to reach out to me at:

hello@DervishMentoring.com.

Good luck!

Learn more about how Dervish Dervish can help your school here